NOAH

A RIGHTEOUS MAN
in a
WICKED AGE

NOAH

A RIGHTEOUS MAN
in a
WICKED AGE

BRUCE A. McDOWELL

Advancing the Ministries of the Gospel
AMG *Publishers*

God's Word to you is our highest calling.

NOAH: A Righteous Man in a Wicked Age

Copyright © 2004 by Bruce A. McDowell
Published by AMG Publishers
6815 Shallowford Rd.
Chattanooga, Tennessee 37421

ISBN 0-89957-143-3

First printing—February 2004

Cover designed by ImageWright, Inc., Chattanooga, Tennessee
Interior design and typesetting by Reider Publishing Services, West Hollywood, California
Edited and Proofread by Agnes Lawless, Dan Penwell, Warren Baker, and Sharon Neal

Printed in the United States of America
10 09 08 07 06 05 04 –EB– 8 7 6 5 4 3 2 1

To Susan,

my helpmate and life partner,
given to me by the LORD
so that we might glorify him
and exalt him together.

Contents

Foreword

By Richard D. Phillips

I CAN THINK OF few things more appropriate than for Bruce McDowell to write a book on the great salvation story of Noah and the Flood. I say this because Bruce is a gifted evangelist to the nations, both as people flock to his center city ministry and as he travels across the globe with the good news of a Savior for all the world.

Noah, like Bruce McDowell, was a great multicultural evangelist, with much to say to our fractured world today. Just as he was the father of all who walk the earth so that all men, women, and children find their origin in him, Noah's place in redemptive history comes before God's covenant became particularized in the line of Abraham. There is no people, race, or religion that may write him off as the product of a rival imagination. And there is no people, no civilization that does not look back into its own history and remember the great Flood and the savior through whom humankind passed into safety. Who better, then, to return the nations—his own children—

to the God and Father of us all than Noah? And who better to renew a dialogue of peace among the fractured races of humanity, than the forebearer in whom we find a shared identity and common bond? If anyone knows the truth about God and what is the hope for the world, it must be Noah. All must come and listen to him.

Noah, then, is a figure to whom all may come on equal ground. And what we learn from him is of the greatest significance, as Bruce McDowell so expertly reveals in this book. It is of Noah that the Bible first uses the term *righteous*. What, then, does it mean to stand in a right relationship to God? Noah can tell us. Similarly, it is in God's dealing with the arkbuilder that we first read the word *grace*. What does it mean that God would look down on a sinful world in grace? We find out in the story of Noah. Noah's Flood provides a great symbol of God's judgment on sin and a warning of a greater judgment yet to come. His ark provides a great type of salvation, as the apostle Peter revealed (1 Pet. 3:20), and his rainbow endures as a symbol of God's covenant promise that means hope for all the world.

Noah shows us the truth of people in sin, revealing not (as some would have it) a wicked, childish God in need of refinement but a wicked, selfish race in need of a Savior to break the clouds and provide a greater ark for a greater judgment. If the problem of sin is what caused judgment in Noah's day and if sin abides in us still, then God's dealings with Noah provide a pattern for what will come again, both in judgment and salvation. Noah teaches us, then, how to hear and obey the call of God unto salvation, even in a world that is bent on evil and destruction.

Here, therefore, is a story that involves us all and speaks to our most basic predicament. Noah shares a distinction with Adam, that every single human being is one of his descendants and may rightly look to him for hope and truth. He shares, as well, a distinction with Jesus Christ. Noah labored on the ark to provide a place of safety for those who heard his call. So also did Jesus, the true carpenter of our salvation, the true Second Adam of whom Noah is but a type, erect the cross, through which all who believe may pass into the clear skies of God's eternal favor and love. I know of no one better qualified to tell this story to all people and to show us how to speak biblically across the barriers our sinful world has made than my longtime friend and colleague, Bruce McDowell.

For all these reasons, this book on Noah and the biblical story of judgment and salvation that came through him is an ideal study for any budding evangelist. If you want to recognize a brother or sister in every face of every shape and color, then listen to the heart of Bruce McDowell. If you want to know how to speak the Bible's story of redemption to every person, then remember the story of our father Noah. May God himself bless these studies to the heart of every reader so that all might know the salvation foretold and promised through Noah and now revealed through our Lord Jesus Christ. And may God call more servants from all the clans of Noah into his vocation to be preachers of righteousness and heralds of a salvation from the wrath to come.

Richard D. Phillips is senior minister of First Presbyterian Church (PCA) in Coral Springs/Margate, Florida. He is speaker-at-large for the Alliance of Confessing Evangelicals, directs the Philadelphia Conference on Reformation Theology, and is Vice Chairman of Reformation Societies International.

Phillips is the author of numerous books, including *Chosen in Christ*, *Turning Your World Upside Down*, and *Turning Back the Darkness*. He and his wife, Sharon, live in South Florida with their four children.

Acknowledgments

I WOULD LIKE to thank Tenth Presbyterian Church for the sabbatical and study leave time afforded to me enabling me to work on writing this book. I thank God for the privilege of preaching the beginning of this work at the worship services of Tenth International Fellowship.

A special thank-you goes to Agnes C. Lawless for her detailed editorial work, to Howard Vos for his editorial comments, and to Sharon Neal and Warren Baker for their superb job of proofreading. And I especially thank my assistant, Geri Secrest, for her valuable help with the indexes. I thank the Lord for each of you.

I appreciated the enthusiasm and encouragement of my writing by Dan Penwell, AMG's new product and acquisitions manager.

Most of all, I thank my wife Susan for her long-suffering and sacrifice with this project that at times seemed endless.

Introduction

THE IMPORTANCE of Noah and the Flood account is indicated in Scripture by the amount of space dedicated to it. Just the account of the Deluge (Gen. 6:9—8:22) covers as much in the Genesis narrative as the millennia from Adam to Noah (4:1—6:8) or from Noah to Abraham (9:1—11:26). The call of Noah, similar to the call of Abraham, indicates the importance of his place in the history of God's redemption of humanity. His life covers the transition from one major epoch to the next in God's dealings with humankind. Noah is one of various patriarchs who were a type of Christ. His life and ministry are in the Scriptures to bless us. As Solomon said,

> The memory of the righteous will be a blessing,
> but the name of the wicked will rot. (Prov. 10:7)

With the rise of higher criticism of the Scriptures, particularly of the Pentateuch, in the late nineteenth and early twentieth centuries, many consider the Flood account to be simply myth and folklore,

similar to pagan mythology. Much attention in recent years among
evangelical Christians has focused on the extent of the Flood, its significance to the antiquity of humanity and the earth, and the explo-
ration of Mount Ararat to find the remains of the ark. Although these
are interesting subjects (I will address the extent of the Flood), the
focus of this study is on the place of Noah in redemptive history and
the account's typology of Christ and our salvation. This is the purpose for which it has been preserved as Scripture. Assuming this to
be true presupposes that the account of Noah and the Flood was not
just a myth but an accurate record of an historical event. Jesus' and
Peter's references to Noah and the Flood as historical gives us author-
itative support for this viewpoint.

The biblical account of the Flood with Noah entering the ark
with the pairs of animals is one of the best known in the whole Bible.
It is often one of the first Bible stories young children learn in
Sunday school. Usually the focus is on the Flood, the animals, and
the rainbow. Most Christian adults hear little if any preaching or
teaching on the account of Noah. Some find it hard to see its relevance to our lives and faith today. As people reread the account as
adults, they are often shocked by the holocaust and the view of God
they may perceive from it. With the violence and depravity portrayed, the account seems more for adults than young children. As
Karen Armstrong remarks, "The stories we hear when we are very,
very young are formative. Whatever we say afterward and however
we try to qualify them with nice, uplifting theology or subtle ideas,
the hideous story of Noah, with God wiping out humanity, remains
in many people's minds. And many people like that kind of God."[1]

Numerous views concerning the main thrust of this long
account may be found from each one's personal background. Some
of those ideas may be enumerated as follows from a discussion moderated by Bill Moyers:

(1) A newspaper journalist sees its message as saying God has
promised in the covenant not to destroy us all again nor will he "be

examining each of us individually as to how we live our lives and develop our faith."

(2) God is developing and learning. As a religion writer who was formerly a nun says, "We start off with an infantile God, knocking down His sand castles—a regretful God Who learns maturity and in the process brutalizes humanity—which then passes on the burden of suffering to other people."

(3) A Jewish seminary professor summarizes it this way: By looking at God, we see that no matter how terribly we fail, even in God's creating the universe, we have a chance to start over. A rainbow is at the end.

(4) A Roman Catholic biblical scholar says that despite humanity's waywardness, God still has faith in human beings. He has decided to relate to a chosen people by a covenant with a universal message. But this story is horrendous in its implications.

(5) A Jewish writer and poetess says there is life after destruction and a chance to rebuild. "There is an ongoing relationship between God and humanity that will never be broken. . . . The covenantal relationship between God and humanity is a paradigm for relationship between human beings."

(6) An African-American theologian sees it this way: After all the devastation with bloated bodies, there is the rainbow and the cloud. That gives us hope by which we can live.

(7) A clinical psychologist sees the account as teaching that God learns humans are vulnerable. He assaults their humanness. God learns that terror and destruction don't change things because evil comes back. The covenant is a two-way relationship so that "the creation of the human world has the potential to reveal things to God, too. . . .[2] I see this story as the education or development of God."[3]

All these explanations fall short of the major truths conveyed in this important portion of Scripture. Some are even blasphemous to our eternal, unchanging God who is always good. A major reason for this is the failure to interpret the text from a Christocentric perspective.

Jesus affirmed the Genesis account as Scripture that testifies of him. As Jesus defended his ministry to the Jews, he said, "You diligently study the Scriptures because you think that by them you possess eternal life. These are the Scriptures that testify about me, yet you refuse to come to me to have life. . . . If you believed Moses, you would believe me, for he wrote about me" (John 5:39, 40, 46).

Luke gave us Jesus' interpretive key to the Old Testament when he met the two men on the road to Emmaus after his resurrection. "And beginning with Moses and all the Prophets, he explained to them what was said in all the Scriptures concerning himself" (Luke 24:27). A short time later, Jesus said to his disciples, "Everything must be fulfilled that is written about me in the Law of Moses, the Prophets and the Psalms" (Luke 24:44). This indicates that the entire Old Testament testified of Jesus and is fulfilled through him. Philip affirmed this as he introduced Nathanael to Jesus. "Philip found Nathanael and told him, 'We have found the one Moses wrote about in the Law, and about whom the prophets also wrote—Jesus of Nazareth, the son of Joseph'" (John 1:45).

As we study the relationship between God and Noah, we see a clear message of the gospel in the light of Christ. This is the approach to the text taken by the ancient church fathers. Andrew Louth says, "This practice of making the text of Scripture shine like a beam of light, as it were, through the prism of faith in Christ, in whom Adam's sin and ours is canceled and in whom the hopes of Israel and the whole of humankind have been fulfilled, is perhaps, to begin with, the strangest thing about the [Church] Fathers' approach to Scripture."[4] This approach may be strange to those trained in a liberal interpretation of the Scriptures, but it was also the approach of the reformers of the sixteenth century and those who have followed that tradition. I have followed that same tradition in this book. It may be summarized as follows:

The conflict between the Seed of the woman and the seed of the serpent (Gen. 3:15) came to a crisis point. The effects of the Fall in the corruption, violence, and destruction of family were widely evident throughout humanity. This deeply grieved the LORD. Because of this, God in his holiness determined to justly destroy all but righteous Noah and his family in an act of redemptive judgment. He made a covenant of preservation with them that they would be delivered through the ordeal of water. This becomes a type of our salvation seen in the new covenant through Christ.

Types are frequently found throughout the Old Testament of New Testament concepts or the work of the three persons of the one God, especially of Christ. A type is a person, thing, or an event that models or symbolizes what will appear later. Most of the types in Genesis find their fulfillment in Christ's person or in his ministry.

Three stages of Noah's life may also be seen as stages of a Christian's spiritual life in regeneration: first, being in the world that is to be judged for its sin but remaining undefiled by it in Christ's righteousness; second, going through the waters of judgment and being separated from the old world; and third, coming out of the ark to enter the cleansed new world of resurrection life and joyful liberty.[5]

Noah was called righteous only because of his relationship with God by grace. He was a type of Christ in his walk with God, in his prophetic role, and in his representation before God of his family, just as Christ represents the family of God before the Father. Evidence of Noah's faith is seen in how he acted on it by building the ark.

The ark became a type of the cosmic kingdom of God; by entering, one is saved from judgment. Entrance through the one door to the ark illustrates how salvation is found only in Christ. Closure of the door by the LORD indicates that God is the chief actor in all these events. He seals us in our salvation. He was present with Noah and spoke to him. He separated and protected his own from the world. Deliverance through the Flood becomes a type of our baptism and salvation as believers in Christ. The Flood itself is a prototype of the redemptive judgment yet to come on the world at the end of the age through the ordeal of fire. It will be redemptive for the elect and damning for the wicked who refuse to submit to Christ's lordship. Jesus will judge humanity, Satan, and the demonic angels who have rebelled against him.

The extent of the Flood was universal, indicating God's glorious triumph over his enemies, yet showing mercy to his elect. In Christ the elect are saved, as were those in the ark, while all around people are left to judgment for their sin. The same word of God that created the universe also brought about the Flood and is preparing to destroy the earth with fire. Therefore, God warns us to flee the coming judgment and destruction of the ungodly by seeking refuge in Christ. Through him we may enter his kingdom ark, by which we may be saved from the flood of judgment.

In remembering Noah after 150 days in the ark, God demonstrated his faithful covenantal love and timely intervention. His remembrance was covenant fulfilling. The wind of the Spirit passed over the earth, making the waters subside and beginning the process of re-creation. The dove sent out who returned with an olive branch reminds us of the new creation made by the Holy Spirit, who transforms the believer to Christlikeness. Noah's coming out of the ark prefigures our union with Christ in passing through judgment to resurrection and new life. We see a new humanity that overcomes evil. God displays his covenantal love toward his elect to accomplish his redemptive purposes.

Upon exiting the ark, Noah offered to God a sacrifice of thanks, homage, and atonement for sin. In faith he offered a sacrifice that prefigured the death of the Seed of Eve who would crush the head of the serpent. He saw by faith "the Lamb that was slain from the creation of the world" (Rev. 13:8). The sweet aroma of sacrifice reminds us that our lives dedicated to the Lord's service are pleasing to God, bringing glory to him (Rom. 12:1).

The sacrifice culminated in God making a covenant with Noah of common grace for the whole world. In this covenant, God renewed his mandate to humanity to fill and rule the earth. In so doing, we fulfill God's purpose to extend his image in people and to glorify his name throughout the earth. This covenant emphasizes the importance of the institution of the family, as the mandate to be fruitful encompasses the other social orders. The prohibition against eating the blood of animals reminds us of the significance of the altar sacrifices, a type of the blood of Christ spilled for our sins. The importance of the image of God in people is emphasized in the prohibition of murder. God gave humankind a share in his judicial authority by the establishment of human government. Jesus was murdered. But through his blood, he purifies us from all sin.

God's covenant rainbow reminds us that God is still good, and he has good in store for us. He is staying his judgment for a while longer to show us his mercy. Noah became the mediator of God's mercy to all creation. He also became a type of the mediatorship of Jesus for our salvation. The rainbow in the clouds points us to the beauty and perfection of God, a reflection of the "sun of righteousness." It reminds God of his promise to never destroy us by flood again and reminds us that he is truly here for us, patiently waiting. This gives us comfort. It is a sign of common grace for all humanity until the final redemption of the covenant community.

Although Noah was a preacher of righteousness who walked with God, no saint is immune from falling into sin. In our spiritual walk, we find we are in a spiritual battle that wars within and without us. As Noah lay drunk and naked in his tent, Shem and Japheth covered him with a garment. Their action was a type of the gracious work of Christ who covers our shame and nakedness through his atonement on the cross. Noah's curse on Canaan should be understood as part of God's judgment on Satan, who sought to destroy the faithful remnant family. Noah's prophetic blessing on his sons anticipated the blessings of the gospel that will go to all nations, tribes, and peoples. We see God's redemptive purposes being accomplished throughout the flow of biblical history. God is sovereignly in control so that his name may be glorified in all the earth.

My hope and prayer is that through an accurate understanding of this portion of God's Word, you will be encouraged in your walk with him.

> A *Peanuts* cartoon pictured Lucy and Linus looking out the window at a steady downpour of rain. "Boy," said Lucy, "look at it rain. What if it floods the whole world?"
>
> "It will never do that," Linus replied confidently. "In the ninth chapter of Genesis, God promised Noah that would never happen again, and the sign of the promise is the rainbow."
>
> "You've taken a great load off my mind," said Lucy with a relieved smile.
>
> "Sound theology," pontificated Linus, "has a way of doing that!"[6]

The account of Noah reminds us of God's promise in a proverb of Solomon:

> When the storm has swept by, the wicked are gone,
>> but the righteous stand firm forever. (Prov. 10:25)

May the Lord find us unmovable in our faith as we follow a great hero who was righteous in a wicked generation.

Notes

1. Bill Moyers, *Genesis: A Living Conversation,* ed. Betty Sue Flowers (New York: Doubleday, 1996), 151.

2. These views are found in ibid., 151–153.

3. Ibid., 140.

4. Andrew Louth, ed., *Genesis 1–11, OT* vol. 1 of *Ancient Christian Commentary on Scripture* (Downers Grove, Ill.: InterVarsity, 2001), xlviii.

5. Andrew Jukes, *Types in Genesis* (Grand Rapids: Kregel, 1976), 105.

6. Michael P. Green, ed., *Illustrations for Biblical Preaching* (Grand Rapids: Baker, 1989), 113.

Humanity's Descent

Genesis 6:1–4

1 *When men began to increase in number on the earth and daughters were born to them,* 2 *the sons of God saw that the daughters of men were beautiful, and they married any of them they chose.* 3 *Then the* LORD *said, "My Spirit will not contend with man forever, for he is mortal; his days will be a hundred and twenty years."*

4 *The Nephilim were on the earth in those days—and also afterward—when the sons of God went to the daughters of men and had children by them. They were the heroes of old, men of renown.*

I**N THE GENEALOGY** of Genesis 5, Moses concluded his account with Noah being born to Lamech. Noah's name implied that he would bring comfort in the labor and painful toil of the ground due to the curse. After living five hundred years, Noah became the father of three sons.

At this point, we come to a transition in the account of early history from the genealogy of the godly line of Seth back to a reminder of the wicked ways of the Cainite line described in chapter 4 (vv. 17–24). Due to abnormal marriages, violent people filled the earth. A universally corrupt race was characterized by indulgent sensuality and heartless cruelty. Now we come to the apex of demonized royal power being exploited in abominations that brought down God's judgment. He did this to preserve a line through whom our Savior would descend. Although Christ preached to people through Noah, they refused to repent. This provided a background as to why God brought judgment on the world.

∼ The Sons of God

"When men began to increase in number on the earth and daughters were born to them, the sons of God saw that the daughters of men were beautiful, and they married any of them they chose" (Gen. 6:1, 2). There are three main views of the meaning of this verse, each of which can be defended linguistically. The first view sees the intermarriage of the "sons of God" with the "daughters of men" as a spiritual corruption of Seth's blessed family line by Cain's cursed line. It is a view held by many prominent theologians, including church fathers Chrysostom and Augustine and reformers Luther and Calvin. This view fits the preceding context of the contrast made between the two genealogical lines. However, it does not adequately explain how "daughters of men" refers to Cainite women. In verses 1 and 2, "daughters" and "men" refer to the human race as a whole.

The second view is that the "sons of God" were fallen angels who corrupted the human race. This is the earliest Jewish interpretation of this passage. In the Book of Job, fallen angels, called "sons of God" in the Hebrew, along with Satan, presented themselves before the LORD (Job 1:6; 2:1). They then created havoc, chaos, and pain for Job, seeking to have him deny his faith in God. Three New Testament passages seem to speak to this time period of Noah when angels were sent to hell and are being held in darkness and chains until the great day of judgment (1 Pet. 3:18–22; 2 Pet. 2:4, 5; Jude 6, 7). But no direct connection was made here with the "sons of God" other than the time period of Noah. However, "sons of God" was translated "angels" by the translators of the Septuagint and other Jewish writers prior to the time of Christ. The pseudepigraphic book of First Enoch, written sometime in the first two centuries BC, speaks of "children of heaven" as angels who have sexual relations with beautiful daughters of men. Both Jude and Second Peter refer to this book. Since Jude quoted from First Enoch (1:9; 60:8) in verses 14 and 15, would he not also be referring to angels in the same way as that book in verse 6? There it says, "And the angels who did not keep their positions of authority but abandoned their own home—these he has kept in darkness, bound with everlasting chains for judgment on the great Day."

Another important point on interpreting Genesis 6 in supernatural terms is that Jude 7 connected the judgment of fallen angels with the judgment that fell on Sodom and Gomorrah. In Sodom the men of the city tried to have sexual relations with the angels appearing as men who had visited Abraham and then Lot. The men of Sodom were described as "having given themselves over to sexual immorality and gone after strange flesh" (Jude 7 NKJV). These men repeated the sin of the angels of Genesis 6 who similarly desired sexual relationships with women.[1]

The problem with this view of "sons of God" is that it seems to be contradicted by Jesus' statement: "When the dead rise, they will neither marry nor be given in marriage; they will be like the angels in heaven" (Mark 12:25). It also seems irrational to the modern mind to think of angels having sexual relations with women. But in response, those who advocate this view point out that this is not equivalent to saying that angels are sexless or could not have sexual relations (Gen. 19:1, 5). In heaven we will still have our identities, including our sexual identities. Although angels do not marry in heaven, it does not mean they did not do so when cast out of heaven.

Another objection to this view is, although we are told in these New Testament passages that fallen angels will be judged, why is the focus in Genesis 6 on men who were flesh (v. 3) and their coming judgment (vv. 5–7) rather than on the "sons of God," that is, angels? However, the passage does refer to their offspring as men, the Nephilim, and their exploits. Yet one is left not completely satisfied with this view.

The third view is that the "sons of God" were tyrannical kings, successors to Cainite Lamech. The Jewish rabbis of the second century AD advocated this view, but it lacks as much ancient support as the other views.[2] *The sons of God* could be translated "the sons of the gods." Ancient texts reveal a belief in divine kings who were children of various gods. This was the belief in ancient Egypt and even in twentieth century Japan in Shintoism. This blasphemous ancient cult of the kings was a further development of the desire of the Cainite line to make a name for itself (cf. Gen. 4:17). The beautiful women they married were just daughters of humans in general. In mentioning that "they married any of them they chose" (Gen. 6:2), we see they were polygamous, as was Lamech (Gen. 4:19), who gathered a harem.[3]

Probably the best understanding of this passage is to combine the last two views to say that the descendants of these men and women who married were the spiritual children of Satan who were given their royal power by demons.[4] When God cursed the serpent in the garden he said, "And I will put enmity between you and the woman, and between your offspring and hers" (Gen. 3:15). These "sons of god" describe the serpent's offspring—demonized humans who assumed dynastic powers and called themselves "gods."

Satan continues to subvert the human race, seeking to draw people to himself against God. Satan is not only against God but also against us who are made in God's image. Satan succeeded in turning Cain into a murderer but failed to destroy the godly line through which would come a deliverer. A remnant family still remained, but they were now persecuted. A great conflict has been in process since the Fall until today for the ultimate possession of the world. We see Satan's challenge to Jesus during his temptation in the wilderness when "the devil took him to a very high mountain and showed him all the kingdoms of the world and their splendor. 'All this I will give you,' he said, 'if you will bow down and worship me' " (Matt. 4:8, 9).

Satan failed in his attempt to destroy the godly family line. God judged that entire corrupted race in the Flood and bound the demonic spirits in hell to await judgment (Jude 6; 2 Pet. 2:4). In doing that, he preserved the human race through righteous Noah and his family. God continued to provide a way for the Messiah to come and save his people. If Satan had been successful, no one from Adam to us could be saved. It was only through the coming of Jesus Christ as our deliverer that we could be saved. So through God's judgment on the corrupted race and his binding of the infiltrating demons, God made possible our eternal salvation. By the victory of Christ's resurrection, we look forward to a new heaven and a new earth (2 Pet. 3:13), an inheritance that can never perish, spoil, or fade (1 Pet. 1:4). At the consummation of the kingdom of God on Christ's return, heavenly voices will loudly proclaim,

> "The kingdom of the world has become the kingdom of our Lord
> and of his Christ,
> and he will reign for ever and ever." (Rev. 11:15)

War will erupt in heaven when the ancient serpent, Satan, and his angels will be cast down to the earth. Then a loud voice in heaven will say,

"Now have come the salvation and the power and the kingdom of
    our God,
    and the authority of his Christ.
For the accuser of our brothers,
    who accuses them before our God day and night,
    has been hurled down.
They overcame him
    by the blood of the Lamb
    and by the word of their testimony." (Rev. 12:10, 11)

～ Humanity's Mortality

The LORD limited a human's days on the earth when he said, "His
days will be a hundred and twenty years" (Gen. 6:3). But in what
sense are we to understand this? Did this mean that people would
only live another 120 years before the destructive Flood or that they
would only live to be 120 years old? Many commentators may be
found on either side of this interpretation.

Taking the view that people would only live 120 years may be
discerned from a study of the context of the passage. When we look
at what comes before and after this verse, we see in Genesis 5:2 that
God created a male and a female and called them "man" (Adam),
referring to humankind. From there the author went from speaking
of humankind to specific men, Adam and his descendants. Now in
Genesis 6:3, the author returned to speaking of "humankind" as God
made his declaration. The long lives of the ten great men listed in the
genealogy were in stark contrast to the 120 years of "humankind."

When the LORD said, "My Spirit will not contend with man forever," it is difficult to know the exact meaning of *contend*. It may be
translated "strive," "rule," or "prevail" according to some. Others
translate it as "abide" or "remain," particularly favored by the
Septuagint and Syriac versions and by its context (giving a contrast
to "his days will be a hundred and twenty years"). If one understands

it to mean "remain," it implies that God's Spirit gave these men mentioned in the genealogy long lives, not by their own strength. But that was the reality of a previous age. Those ten men were exceptions rather than the rule. Now people were to live no longer than 120 years. It indicates the reality of the Fall and our separation from our Creator. The author continued to give the ages of men in the subsequent genealogy (11:10–26), showing a dramatic decline in their ages. The Pentateuch (books of Moses) ends with Moses dying at exactly 120 years while he still had good eyesight and strength (Deut. 34:7).[5] But his death was punishment for his disobedience in the wilderness in hitting the rock (Num. 20:7–12). As the meekest man in the earth, he still went the way of all humanity, dying for his sin. Thus, human mortality was emphasized. God made a contrast between the Spirit abiding with people forever and stating that they are mortal or flesh. People are incurably carnal, sensual, and corrupt. Because God is holy, the Holy Spirit cannot continue to be with unholy men and women. Since the Holy Spirit sustained the lives of people for so long, the removal of the Spirit shortened their life spans.

The LORD spoke of our mortality through Isaiah saying,

"All men are like grass,
    and all their glory is like the flowers of the field.
The grass withers and the flowers fall,
    because the breath of the LORD blows on them.
    Surely the people are grass.
The grass withers and the flowers fall,
    but the word of our God stands forever." (Isa. 40:6–8)

Our lives are short, but we behave like we will live forever. We take no thought for tomorrow. But we don't know what tomorrow holds—life or death. "Now is the day of salvation" (2 Cor. 6:2). Are we prepared to face our own death? The only way to face the future in complete peace is to have peace with God through our Lord Jesus Christ. Then he will give us the peace that passes all understanding. It is a peace that comes with knowing that we will not face judgment, for our sins are washed away and forgiven.

But the men and women of Noah's day did not have that peace and hope. They thought they were masters of their own destinies. They did whatever they saw fit, even if they crushed and abused those who got in the way of achieving their power and name-recognition lust.

As believers we must forsake that lifestyle. John reminded us of this:

> Do not love the world or anything in the world. If anyone loves the world, the love of the Father is not in him. For everything in the world—the cravings of sinful man, the lust of his eyes and the boasting of what he has and does—comes not from the Father but from the world. The world and its desires pass away, but the man who does the will of God lives forever. (1 John 2:15–17)

Note that last sentence: "The world and its desires pass away." Such worldliness characterized the "sons of the gods" and the "daughters of men." They soon passed away in judgment by God. In contrast, "the man who does the will of God lives forever."

Although life for people on earth was now greatly shortened, there was the possibility of never dying. Enoch, the seventh from Adam, was an example of this (Gen. 5:24). Although we will someday die physically, those of us who know God, love him, and live for him, we will never die spiritually. We will live forever and be given new resurrected bodies. What a wonderful hope we accept by faith because Christ rose from the dead!

In support of the view that the Flood would come in 120 years is the fact that in the genealogy of Genesis 11:10–32, all the men named lived over 120 years, although there was a steep decline in the years they lived. Ages range from Shem, who lived six hundred years to Nahor, who lived 148 years. Even Abraham lived to 175 years (Gen. 25:7). After this period of the patriarchs, people's lives declined further until they leveled off. As Moses wrote, "The length of our days is seventy years—or eighty, if we have the strength" (Ps. 90:10). But in modern times an occasional person lives to the age of 120.

When the LORD said, "My Spirit will not contend with man forever," we see the withdrawal of God's life-giving Spirit within 120 years. This was a sign of judgment and a return to the primordial conditions of Genesis 1:2 when "the earth was formless and empty, darkness was over the surface of the deep" before the re-creation after the Flood. Even for those who lived extremely long lives, the Spirit did not abide with them *forever*. So this cannot confirm a decrease in humanity's life span.

The Spirit contended with the people of Noah's generation by preaching the gospel to them through Noah. Isaiah testified of Christ saying, "From the beginning I have not spoken in secret, from the time it came to be I have been there" (Isa. 48:16 ESV). Christ's Spirit openly made the gospel known to the wicked people in Noah's day. However, he would not continue to make fruitless exhortations without limit. Only for a period of 120 years the Spirit of Christ would call people to repentance and patiently hold back his wrath.

Genesis 6:3 says that humans are "mortal," or "flesh." God contradicted the pretensions to deity of the "sons of the gods," by describing them as men who are only "flesh." Humanity's animal-like mortality was repeatedly emphasized in the context of the judgment to come within 120 years. People seeking to have the status of immortal gods were reduced to the same fate as mortal beasts (cf. Gen. 6:12, 13, 17, 19).

Another confirmation of the view that "120 years" referred to a time of reprieve before the judgment is Genesis 5:32. Noah was five hundred years old when he became the father of Japheth (the eldest; Gen. 10:21), Shem, and Ham (the youngest; Gen. 9:24). Shem was ninety-eight when the Flood came (Gen. 11:10). But Noah was six hundred years old when the floodwaters came on the earth (Gen. 7:6). It seems logical that Noah's children were born in a twenty-some year period between God's declaration of coming destruction (Gen. 6:7) and the birth of Japheth, Shem, and Ham. Shem was born twenty-two years after the pronouncement of coming judgment. So people's days being limited to 120 years was a time of reprieve, a holding back of God's judgment, giving time for them to repent under the preaching of Noah, "a preacher of righteousness" (2 Pet. 2:5). Backing this view is 1 Peter 3:20, "When God waited patiently in the days of Noah while the ark was being built." Could not that period of God's waiting be 120 years?

Actually, the pre-incarnate Christ preached through Noah to that generation (1 Pet. 3:19).[6] The "Spirit of Christ" in the prophet "spoke of the grace that was to come" through predicting the "sufferings of Christ and the glories that would follow" (1 Pet. 1:10, 11). Christ's preaching through Noah of Christ's death and resurrection was demonstrated in type by the deliverance of Noah and his family through water, illustrating the antitype of baptism. Baptism in part symbolizes our salvation by Christ's death and resurrection. Noah's building of the ark during those 120 years gave testimony to this salvation. Through Noah, Christ preached a message of faith and repentance so that people would come to him. He preached to those people whose souls, now separated from their bodies (Heb. 12:23), were called "spirits in prison" or hell (1 Pet. 3:19; Rev. 20:7). Peter confirmed again that as a past event "the gospel was preached even to those who are dead" (1 Pet. 4:6 ESV), who had been alive at the time. Therefore, the contemporaries of Noah had no excuse, for he warned them of the coming judgment if they did not repent. But they thought the whole proposition ridiculous and hardened their hearts to Noah's appeal. Similarly today, people follow those who produce miraculous signs, demonstrate worldly power, or speak with the wisdom of this age. But the preaching of the gospel of Christ crucified is a stumbling block and foolishness for the worldly (1 Cor. 1:23).

Building an ark the size of a modern cargo ship took a long time for only four men. Even if they hired many helpers, it would have taken much time to build. Likewise, God patiently gives us time to repent. Although God's mercy is great and he is patient with our sinfulness, yet there is a limit. "Reprieves are not pardons; though God bear a great while, he will not bear always."[7] We must turn to the Lord in repentance now, or judgment will come on us suddenly if we are unprepared (Matt. 24:42–51).

∽ The Nephilim

"The Nephilim were on the earth in those days—and also afterward—when the sons of God went to the daughters of men and had children by them. They were the heroes of old, men of renown" (Gen. 6:4). The Nephilim appear to be powerful tyrant kings. They were heroes in the world's eyes, for they held the world's values. They had made a name for themselves and so were famous. This is what Cain tried to do in naming the city he built after his first son Enoch (Gen. 4:17). It is also what the men who built the Tower of Babel envisioned (Gen. 11:4). Their ambition was to make a name for themselves rather than calling on the name of the LORD. We, however, should glorify God in all we do (1 Cor. 10:31), for whatever we have and are have come from him. "For in him we live and move and have our being" (Acts 17:28).

The author said that the Nephilim were on the earth "and also afterward." This does not necessarily mean that their physical descendants were around but that the demonic spiritual natures and attitudes of these people continued. People's corrupt sinful natures did not change after the Flood. Noah cursed Ham's son Canaan for

Ham's sin (Gen. 9:25). Ham's faithless action led to an ungodly line, which the Israelite army eventually destroyed in Canaan.

After the twelve spies explored the Promised Land of Canaan, ten spies who lacked faith said, " 'The land we explored devours those living in it. All the people we saw there are of great size. We saw the Nephilim there (the descendants of Anak came from the Nephilim). We seemed like grasshoppers in our own eyes, and we looked the same to them' " (Num. 13:32, 33). These faithless words, which discouraged the Israelites, were likely exaggerations. But the Anakites were known to be "strong and tall" (Deut. 9:2). The Nephilim in Canaan and those heroes of old in Noah's day were apparently connected. The people in Canaan were powerful and lived in large, fortified cities (Num. 13:28).[8] The same must have been true of these antediluvian people. They were tyrant kings who concentrated their power through corruption and violence. The Hebrew root of the Nephilim means "to fall," possibly suggesting their ultimate fate. The Nephilim in Noah's day drowned in the Flood. Also all the Canaanite cities fell under Joshua's leadership. Perhaps the giant Og of Bashan was a Nephilim descendant, being a powerful, wicked king with a thirteen-foot-long and six-foot-wide iron bed. He was described as the last of the Rephaites (Deut. 3:11), who must have been a family of giants (Deut. 2:10, 11). Possibly one of the later Nephilim was the Philistine Goliath. The Philistines were also descendants of Ham. The shepherd boy David approached Goliath through his faith, even though the whole Israelite army feared the giant greatly (1 Sam. 17:11, 24, 50). The Nephilim represented Satan's oppressive, corrupt, and violent rule as he tried to destroy God's created order and rule (see Gen. 6:11–13). In the sight of God, the Nephilim were sinners ripe for judgment.

The serpent that appeared in the garden to deceive Eve and Adam still tries to destroy God's creation. We are engaged in a spiritual warfare whose nature is more fully revealed in the New

Testament where the serpent is called the devil or Satan (Rom. 16:20; Rev. 12:9).

There are ranks of power among the fallen angels (Eph. 1:21; 3:10; Col. 1:16). Some appear to embody themselves in certain powerful and evil persons (Acts 13:6–10; 1 John 4:1, 3). These people devote themselves to being slaves of Satan, although it may take all sorts of outward forms. They lead people through deceit into violence and rebellion against authority, destroying families, and oppressing Christians. Often they develop a cultlike following of loyalists who oppose the work of God and the gospel. They are antichrists, of which there will be many through history (1 John 2:18). As believers we must pray against them and their influence so the kingdom of God will advance with power; for God works through our prayers.

As Moses recited a song concerning the Israelites' relationship with God, he said that in worshiping other gods "they sacrificed to demons, which are not God" (Deut. 32:17; cf. Lev. 17:7). If we worship anything other than the one true and living God who created all things, we are worshiping the creation at Satan's bidding.

Some gain great power and strength from demonic worship. Often such worship involves sexual rituals, which invite demons to live in a person's body (Exod. 32:6; Num. 25:1, 2). Other satanic rituals even include offering children as sacrifices to demons (Lev. 20:2–5; 2 Kings 23:10; 2 Chron. 33:6). Those so possessed corrupt and destroy God's good created order. We see this in their distortion of God's design for marriage (Gen. 4:19; 6:2). Then we see it in their corruption of morals and through violence in seeking power (Gen. 4:23, 24; 6:11, 13). The more power they gain the more corrupt and violent they become. In Noah's day their objective was to create a name for themselves as famous warriors and despotic rulers (Gen. 6:4).

In the twentieth century, despotic rulers such as Stalin, Hitler, Mussolini, Hirohito, and Mao Tse-tung tried to destroy the people of God. We see the same being done today throughout the world—just look at the recent rule of Milosevich in Yugoslavia, Charles Taylor in Liberia, Saddam Hussein in Iraq, and Kim Jong Il in North Korea. All allegiances other than to the cult of Kim Jong Il's dead father are not tolerated in North Korea. In the more recent past, Osama bin Laden in Afghanistan, Idi Amin in Uganda, and Pol Pot in Cambodia also tried to destroy any evidence of the kingdom of God.

But the despotic rulers of Noah's day, as those of today, did not recognize the hour at hand. They continued on in their everyday lives as if they were accountable to no one. They could not read the signs in the sky nor recognize the voice of God in the preaching of Noah.

Ever since the fall of Adam and Eve, a spiritual struggle has gone on between light and darkness, good and evil. As Paul wrote, "For our struggle is not against flesh and blood, but against the rulers, against the authorities, against the powers of this dark world and against the spiritual forces of evil in the heavenly realms" (Eph. 6:12). That struggle will continue until the end of the age when Jesus returns in triumph. Then he will have complete victory over his enemies. Satan and his dark angels will be thrown into the lake of burning sulfur to be tormented for ever and ever (Rev. 20:10). We can have confidence that Christ will ultimately triumph over evil.

SCRIPTURE READING:

PSALM 14

Discussion Questions

1. How would you describe the context in which Noah was living before the Flood?
2. Is there a time limit to God's patience with sinners? How did God state that to Noah? How may we take warning from that?

3. Was the gospel preached before the age of the apostles? If so, how was it preached through Noah?

4. Who were the Nephilim and the "sons of the gods"? What was their apparent role in society?

5. How do we see evidence of demonic influence in today's corrupt society?

6. Are we in a period of God patiently waiting before he brings sudden judgment?

7. What is our hope for the future in light of the grim reality of evil all around us?

Notes

1. James Montgomery Boice, *Genesis,* vol. 1 of *An Expositional Commentary* (Grand Rapids: Zondervan, 1982), 244–248.

2. R. C. Sproul, ed., *New Geneva Study Bible* (Nashville: Thomas Nelson, 1995), 18.

3. Meredith G. Kline, "Genesis," in *The New Bible Commentary,* eds. D. Guthrie and J. A. Motyer (Grand Rapids: Eerdmans, 1970), 87.

4. Sproul, *New Geneva Study Bible,* 18.

5. John H. Sailhamer, "Genesis," in vol. 2 of *The Expositor's Bible Commentary,* ed. Frank E. Gaebelein (Grand Rapids: Zondervan, 1990), 76–78.

6. Today Christ preaches to the world through us as we preach the Word of Christ, the gospel (John 10:16; Rom. 10:17).

7. Matthew Henry, *An Exposition of the Old and New Testament,* vol. 1 (Philadelphia: Towar, J. & D. M. Hogan, 1830), 60.

8. The cities were thought to be larger because they were set on hills and appeared to be walled to heaven.

The LORD Is Grieved

Genesis 6:5–8

5 *The LORD saw how great man's wickedness on the earth had become, and that every inclination of the thoughts of his heart was only evil all the time.* **6** *The LORD was grieved that he had made man on the earth, and his heart was filled with pain.* **7** *So the LORD said, "I will wipe mankind, whom I have created, from the face of the earth—men and animals, and creatures that move along the ground, and birds of the air—for I am grieved that I have made them."* **8** *But Noah found favor in the eyes of the LORD.*

A PART FROM God's revelation to us, we do not realize the depth of our sin and wickedness in his sight. In these verses, we are confronted with our radical departure from God's righteousness and its affront to his perfection. So the concluding eight verses (Gen. 6:1–8) of the book of Adam (Gen. 5:1) tell us why God had to judge the world as described in the book of Noah

(Gen. 6:9–9:29). But in the midst of God's terrible pronouncement of judgment, his loving grace was on Noah, which gives us hope.

∼ Human Wickedness

"The LORD saw how great man's wickedness on the earth had become, and that every inclination of the thoughts of his heart was only evil all the time" (Gen. 6:5). Here we have a contrast made between what the LORD saw when he completed his creation and what resulted from the Fall in the garden. After creating the universe, the plants, the animals, and humans, "God saw all that he had made, and it was very good" (Gen. 1:31). But now God was grieved by what he saw of man's wickedness. It was very great wickedness on the part of all but Noah.

The words describing man's condition "that *every* inclination of the thoughts of his heart was *only* evil *all* the time" convince us that in God's sight we are sinful to the core. It is a comprehensive statement of the depth of our corruption. It does not mean that we continually commit as much sin as possible but that our very nature is to think, say, and do evil. Even our good works do not please God, for they are not done to glorify him. Even after the Flood, God said of man that "every inclination of his heart is evil from childhood" (Gen. 8:21). So human nature did not change after the Flood. People did not become better. Paul quoted the Psalms regarding our degenerate spiritual state:

> "There is no one righteous, not even one;
>> there is no one who understands,
>> no one who seeks God.
> All have turned away,
>> they have together become worthless;
> There is no one who does good,
>> not even one." (Rom. 3:10–12)

We all have thoughts that are continually inclined toward evil. Only a radical change of heart by the Holy Spirit enables us to have new natures.

In the sixteenth century, Martin Luther had a famous debate with Erasmus of Rotterdam on the extent of people's sinful natures. Luther used verse five of our text to great effect in his arguments against Erasmus. Erasmus, as those of the Arminian theological position, believed that although all men and women are sinners, they have enough good in them to use their free wills to turn from sin and believe in Christ, thus being saved. Luther taught that our wills are bound, unable to repent and chose Christ because of our sinful natures. We can do nothing but sin. The "good" we do by God's common grace is only a relative good that has absolutely no merit. It is actually sinful because it is not done for the glory of God. We are saved only because of God's enabling grace through the Holy Spirit, which enlightens our minds and turns our hearts to the Lord. When we see the depths of our sin, we realize our complete inability to contribute toward our salvation. Our despair at our situation should move us to call on God for his mercy. Only then do we give all the glory to God for his revealed righteousness through Jesus Christ. Jonathan Edwards, America's greatest theologian and preacher, taught the same in his book *The Freedom of the Will* as he refuted eighteenth-century humanists and deists.

The seriousness of the extent of humankind's sin as described in the Bible is a stumbling block for humanists, Muslims, Hindus, and Buddhists. Roman Catholics reject it as too pessimistic. As the Dutch theologian Berkouwer wrote, "Scripture constantly makes it clear that sin is not something which corrupts relatively or partially, but a corruption which fully affects the radix, the root, of man's existence, and therefore man himself."[1] The power of sin is like an avalanche, overwhelming all obstacles in its way. Our perverse hearts are evident in the way they affect all our relationships. This state of radical corruption is referred to in the Gospels as being lost. Our hearts are alienated from the life of God. We cannot escape this lost-ness until God seeks us and finds us (Isa. 65:1; Luke 15:3–10; 19:10; John 6:44; cf. Rom. 10:20).

Only as we understand the seriousness of our sin in light of God's holiness can we understand the justice of God in bringing destruc-tion on humanity. Anselm of Canterbury, appointed archbishop of England in 1093, said that "if anyone imagines that God can simply forgive us, that person has 'not yet considered what a heavy weight sin is.' "[2] James Boice describes sin as "an infinite offense against God's utterly upright character."[3] The only solution to this dilemma of humanity's condition is found in the God-man, Jesus Christ, who satisfied the justice of God at the cross through his shed blood for sinners. Noah passing through judgment entombed in the ark pic-tures that satisfaction for sin in type.

~ The LORD's Grief

"The LORD was grieved that he had made man on the earth" (Gen. 6:6). As an anthropomorphic expression, the LORD was dis-tressed by the perversion of his creative purpose for humanity. A strange reversal took place in our proper roles. Rather than acknowl-edging God as Lord and King, people became lords and kings, as exemplified in the Nephilim giants described in verse 4. As Meredith Kline points out, "In the strange cult of man, sinners are deified and God does the repenting!"[4]

This verse does not teach us that God made a mistake or changed his mind because he did not foresee what was going to hap-pen. He did not make a mistake in creating humanity. God is not surprised by anything nor does he change his plans because things happen over which he has no control. He was not surprised by the development of sin in humanity. God is sovereign, knowing the end from the beginning of all things. He created time; so all things are eternally present for him. He has an eternal purpose that does not change, yet remains a mystery to us. It was within God's eternal plan that he would send Jesus to die for sinners (Eph. 1:4, 5; Rev. 13:8).

God is a personal God who responds to us. He is a God with feeling who responds to our thoughts and actions. He feels sorrow because of our sin. Israel "rebelled and grieved his Holy Spirit" (Isa. 63:10). Paul instructed new believers how to live the Christian life and wrote, "And do not grieve the Holy Spirit of God" (Eph. 4:30). Twice in a passage describing how King Saul of Israel disobeyed the LORD, we are told that the LORD was grieved he made Saul king. "Then the word of the LORD came to Samuel: 'I am grieved that I have made Saul king, because he has turned away from me and has not carried out my instructions'" (1 Sam. 15:11). "And the LORD was grieved that he had made Saul king over Israel" (1 Sam. 15:35). These verses indicate that God had a change of attitude and actions toward the people he was dealing with. He responds to changing circumstances in human history in a meaningful way.

This does not mean that God changes his mind. As God spoke through Balaam, "God is not a man, that he should lie, nor a son of man, that he should change his mind" (Num. 23:19; cf. 1 Sam. 15:29). Nor does God's grief mean that he changes. God told us through the prophet Malachi, "I the LORD do not change. So you, O descendants of Jacob, are not destroyed" (Mal. 3:6). Theologians call this attribute of God his immutability. Recently, some theologians who call themselves evangelical have repudiated the belief in God's immutability and sovereignty. They say that God changes in response to us. He doesn't know the future. God is evolving and growing. This teaching is clearly contradictory to the Bible's revelation of God. It is partially based on the process philosophy of people such as Alfred North Whitehead and the theology of John Cobb and springs out of an emphasis on libertarian freedom. But the Bible says, "The plans of the LORD stand firm forever, the purposes of his heart through all generations"

(Ps. 33:11). The LORD says, "No one can deliver out of my hand. When I act, who can reverse it?" (Isa. 43:13).

What we find in various passages concerning God relenting, grieving, or changing his mind (Hebrew *nacham*) is that by his very nature he relents.

> Return to the LORD your God,
> for he is gracious and compassionate,
> slow to anger and abounding in love,
> and he relents from sending calamity.
> Who knows? He may turn and have pity
> and leave behind a blessing. (Joel 2:13, 14)

In passages dealing with God's grieving and being sorry he is described in human terms that relate to our knowledge and emotions. The Bible uses anthropomorphic language to describe him from our human vantage point of living in time on earth.

> We must also recognize that the immutable and sovereign God deals appropriately with changes in human behavior. When they sin or repent of sin, He "changes His mind" with regard to the blessing or punishment appropriate to the situation (Exod. 32:12, 14; 1 Sam. 15:11; 2 Sam. 24:16; Jer. 18:11; Amos 7:3, 6)—all in accordance with His sovereign and eternal purposes. Because God is changeless in His being, and eternally loyal to His covenant promises, we can have firm confidence in Him who is "The same yesterday, today, and forever" (Heb. 13:8).[5]

Therefore, we can be confident of God's love and care even in the midst of suffering and uncertainty.

God relates to us as part of his way of working by relenting. Many of God's prophecies of judgment and blessing are conditional on human response. So God can cancel or reverse his prior-announced decision depending on people's responses. God not only decrees the ends but also the means by which he will accomplish his purposes. Many of God's purposes are achieved through our prayers and actions. God was sorry he had made people on the earth after having declared his creation "very good" when he saw that their "every inclination of the thoughts" of their hearts was "only evil all the time." God was responding to people's conditions in a way that may be described like an actor in history. As John Frame states it, "The author of history has written himself into the play as the lead character, and he interacts with other characters, doing what they do."[6] Being in history in an immanent temporal way, God is in time, changing as do others. Therefore, it is consistent with God's nature and character for him to grieve or be sorry for making people. This is as real as the atemporal, changeless existence of God through which he has eternally decreed what will happen. In his sovereignty, God brings to pass all things according to his will.

"And [God's] heart was filled with pain" (Gen. 6:6). "He was grieved in his heart" (NKJV). Literally, this could be translated as "indignant rage." God was angry with that generation for their perverse sins of corruption and violence. God is a holy God, and sin is totally contrary to his nature. He cannot have sinners in his presence (Hab. 1:13). But after the Flood, Noah offered a burnt offering of clean birds and animals that God received as a soothing aroma (Gen. 8:20, 21). This is a type of the sacrifice of Jesus Christ on the cross, which turns away the wrath of God against our sin. We are saved from the indignant rage of God for our sins because Christ bore them for us. But the people of Noah's generation did not share his faith in God and did not obey him.

Lamech used an interesting play on words in Hebrew in the naming of his son Noah. Lamech said of Noah, "He will comfort us in the labor and painful toil of our hands caused by the ground the LORD has cursed" (Gen. 5:29). When Noah was introduced in Genesis 6:8, he seemed associated with the comfort given to God from the grief and pain associated with human sin. Not only people suffered grief and pain, but God also suffered grief over sin.[7] Noah was associated with the role of comforter, for through him God's plan for glorifying himself in sending a redeemer to save sinners was to be accomplished. The woman's Seed would achieve victory over sin, death, and Satan.

∿ The LORD's Destruction

Noah and his household were the last of the godly people from Seth's line to survive the persecution under the demon-driven, self-deified rulers seeking their elimination. Humanity's rebellion had now reached a crescendo. They repudiated the common grace of allowing both the ungodly and the godly to live together. Because they aspired to world dominion, they refused to extend common grace to those who did not bow to their self-appointed status as gods. In doing this, they shut off the extension of God's common grace to themselves. "By axing common grace they cut off the branch they are sitting on."[8]

Since the faithful remnant was about to be run off the land, the LORD heard their cries for help. "Rise up, O Judge of the earth; pay back to the proud what they deserve. How long will the wicked, O LORD, how long will the wicked be jubilant?" (Ps. 94:2, 3). Their Protector no longer delayed his response to their appeal. They were identified with him in what became a type of baptism and salvation. Through them God's plan for the salvation of humanity would be realized in the fulfillment of the messianic Seed.

God's response was to reverse his creation in order to make a new beginning. In these verses and the following Flood account, a connection is made between the creation account and the Flood in that the effect of "the Flood was a reversal of God's good work of Creation. In chapter 1 God is shown as the one who prepared the good land for man and his family. In the account of the Flood, on the other hand, God is shown as the one who takes this good land from man when he acts corruptly and does not walk in God's way."[9]

God continues to exact just punishment on peoples who rebel against his lordship. He brought sudden destruction on the Assyrian Empire in 612 BC for their brutal cruelty, violence, and pride as prophesied by Nahum. He wrote, "The LORD is good, a refuge in times of trouble. He cares for those who trust in him, but with an overwhelming flood he will make an end of Nineveh; he will pursue his foes into darkness" (Nah. 1:7, 8).

"So the LORD said, 'I will wipe mankind, whom I have created, from the face of the earth'" (Gen. 6:7). The first era of humankind, although created good, would be destroyed because of its wickedness.

Since the Flood, we are in the second era of the earth, which will be destroyed by fire (2 Pet. 3:3–12). The destruction of the earth by flood was a model of the destruction that will come on the ungodly by fire (2 Pet. 3:6, 7). The third era will be the perfect one where everything is made new. Then there will no longer be death, pain, or tears (Rev. 21:4, 5).

From this sudden destruction of humanity by judgment, God wants to teach us to be ready for another sudden destruction that will come on the earth. Jesus' disciples asked him what would be the sign of his coming and the end of the age.

> "No one knows about that day or hour, not even the angels in heaven, nor the Son, but only the Father. As it was in the days of Noah, so it will be at the coming of the Son of Man. For in the days before the flood, people were eating and drinking, marrying and giving in marriage, up to the day Noah entered the ark; and they knew nothing about what would happen until the flood came and took them all away. That is how it will be at the coming of the Son of Man. Two men will be in the field; one will be taken and the other left. Two women will be grinding with a hand mill; one will be taken and the other left.

"Therefore keep watch, because you do not know on what day your Lord will come. But understand this: If the owner of the house had known at what time of night the thief was coming, he would have kept watch and would not have let his house be broken into. So you also must be ready, because the Son of Man will come at an hour when you do not expect him." (Matt. 24:36–44)

Are we ready to meet the Lord? No one knows when he will come again but God the Father. That was set by the Father's own authority (Acts 1:7). Do we fear his judgment, or do we anticipate his warm welcome as we enter his house as his son or daughter? Today is the time to make sure we are prepared to meet our Maker.

~ Earth's Decay

"So the LORD said, 'I will wipe mankind, whom I have created, from the face of the earth—men and animals, and creatures that move along the ground, and birds of the air' " (Gen. 6:7).

The sinfulness of humanity does not just affect ourselves but all of life. All living things are bound together. Adam and Eve's fall affected the whole creation. First, it affected the ground. Because it was cursed, it yielded its crops through painful toil and also produced thorns and thistles (Gen. 3:17, 18). Second, as rulers of the earth and all the creatures on it, humanity's fall into sin also brought judgment on them. People's corrupted rule over the birds and animals caused the creatures to suffer judgment too, even though they were morally innocent.

We see effects of the Fall on many aspects of creation, although how is debated among Bible-believing Christians. Those taking a catastrophic view of the Fall see it in animals devouring one another and suffering death. However, uniformitarians see this as a natural part of the creation order (see Ps. 104:21, 24–30, especially

verse 29 in the context of the description of the days of creation).
The earth splits and shakes in earthquakes, and tornadoes and
typhoons wreak havoc on the earth. One place becomes a flooded
lake and another a parched desert wasteland. Is this due to the
effects of the Fall or to subsequent sin? The prophets frequently
spoke of such events as judgment because of the wickedness of the
people (Ps. 107:33, 34; Isa. 24:1–7; Jer. 50:38; Hag. 1:5–11). But
their wickedness was a result of the Fall.

Paul spoke of creation's subjection to frustration and "bondage
to decay" to the Romans when describing our future glory for which
we hope.

> The creation waits in eager expectation for the sons of God to be
> revealed. For the creation was subjected to frustration, not by its
> own choice, but by the will of the one who subjected it, in hope
> that the creation itself will be liberated from its bondage to decay
> and brought into the glorious freedom of the children of God.
>
> We know that the whole creation has been groaning as in the
> pains of childbirth right up to the present time. (Rom. 8:19–22)

The pain of childbirth was a curse God put on the woman after the
Fall (Gen. 3:16). Personification of creation as in childbirth labor is
thus compared to the present groaning of the earth. But the emphasis is on the future transformation from being in "bondage to decay"
to a "glorious freedom."

This groaning of the earth will end when the Day of the Lord
comes and Jesus brings a new heaven and a new earth (Isa. 65:17;
2 Pet. 3:13; Rev. 21:1), thus renewing all things. Even though most
of the animals were destroyed in the Flood, a remnant was saved to
replenish the earth. This is a type of the renewal and filling that will
come on all the new earth. "The wolf and the lamb will feed
together, and the lion will eat straw like the ox" (Isa. 65:25; cf.
11:6–9). No longer will there be any sea (Rev. 21:1), a symbol of

evil. There will be no night nor will there be the sun or moon for light, for the glory of God and the Lamb will light the new Jerusalem (Rev. 21:23; 22:5). "On each side of the river [of the water of life] stood the tree of life, bearing twelve crops of fruit, yielding its fruit every month. And the leaves of the tree are for the healing of the nations. No longer will there be any curse" (Rev. 22:2, 3). Hallelujah! We have much to look forward to. This is not a return to the Garden of Eden but a place much more glorious and advanced over the limited conditions of Eden.

⌇ Noah Favored

As the black thunderclouds of God's wrath were gathering to rain destruction on the great wickedness of humans (cf. Ps. 18:7–15), a glimmer of sunshine broke through to illuminate the grace of God. The dawn of a new day brought hope in the life of righteous Noah, who walked with God. In contrast to the rest of humanity, only Noah was the recipient of God's grace during those days of wickedness. "But Noah found favor in the eyes of the LORD" (Gen. 6:8). With these words and the mention of Noah at the end of chapter 5 (vv. 29, 32), we are prepared for the account of Noah and the Flood. God's unchanging purpose of fulfilling his promise through the woman's Seed was almost extinguished since only Noah and his family were left. This required a radical change in God's administration of his creation. Thus, he brought down his judgment in the Flood, but he gave Noah grace.

Some translations of the Hebrew word *hen* (חֵן) in this verse use the term *grace* rather than *favor*, such as the New King James Version. This is the first place in the Bible where God's grace is mentioned, although Adam and Eve, Seth, Enoch, and the other patriarchs of Seth's line mentioned were recipients of God's grace. Adam and Eve would have suffered eternal destruction if they were not given God's grace. God also extended his grace to them by promising a Deliverer who would crush the serpent's head. Grace is God's unmerited favor, abundant bounty, given to people as a free gift. As God demonstrated his grace in saving Noah from the Flood, he also later showed his grace in saving Lot from the judgment that came on the cities of Sodom and Gomorrah.

God always reserves a remnant of those who are faithful to him. His promise of a Deliverer would not be abrogated by his destruction of humankind. He would preserve a descendant of Noah through whom the promise would eventually be fulfilled. A remnant was chosen by grace. Those of us who have trusted in Christ alone for our salvation are that believing remnant today. Paul wrote of the remnant at the time of the prophet Elijah.

> So too, at the present time there is a remnant chosen by grace. And if by grace, then it is no longer by works; if it were, grace would no longer be grace.
>
> What then? What Israel sought so earnestly it did not obtain, but the elect did. The others were hardened, as it is written:

> "God gave them a spirit of stupor,
>   eyes so that they could not see
>   and ears so that they could not hear,
> to this very day." (Rom. 11:5–8)

So too in Noah's day the people were in a spiritual stupor, blind and deaf to their sin and rebellion against their holy God. It was not Noah's righteousness and blamelessness (Gen. 6:9) that led to God's grace being on him. Rather, he had that character as a result of God's grace. God saved Noah just as he saves us through his unconditional gift of life. It was purchased by the sacrifice of Christ on the cross. Noah's animal sacrifices (Gen. 8:20) were a type looking forward to the sacrifice of Jesus to cover all sins on the cross. Even though Noah was a sinner like all of us, by God's grace he did not continue to live in sin, but he walked with God. Noah's righteous life and obedience to God, together with his representation before God for his family, made him a type of Christ. Noah and his wife, his three sons and their wives, making eight in all, were saved from the Flood. Christ saves us as he represents the whole family of God before God the Father.

We see in these verses God's characteristic way of dealing with evil. He does not take any half measures. With forcefulness he brought judgment on evil, as will be seen in the coming Flood, and with abundant, unmerited grace he saved Noah and his family from destruction. Thus, in a generation of despair we see a gleam of hope.

The situation is not any different for us today. We all face God's wrath and destruction apart from the grace of God. But in God's mercy, he calls all who hear his message to repent of their sins, turn in faith to Christ for salvation, and submit to his lordship. While we still have opportunity, will we not do so now?

SCRIPTURE READING:
ROMANS 3:9–20

Discussion Questions

1. Are people's spiritual conditions today any different than at the time of Noah? Defend your answer.
2. How does humanity's spiritual condition affect our ability to know and love God?
3. Does God have feelings? If so, how does what we do affect him? Does God change?
4. How can we be ready for the destruction that is soon to come on the earth?
5. After having created all the plants and animals and declared that they were good, how could God change his mind to allow everything but those on the ark to be destroyed?

6. Has the fall had an effect on the whole created order? What will God do on the earth at the end of the age?

7. How does Noah portray Christ and his grace?

Notes

1. G. C. Berkouwer, *Man: The Image of God* (Grand Rapids: Eerdmans, 1962), 140–141.

2. James Montgomery Boice, *Whatever Happened to the Gospel of Grace?* (Wheaton, Ill.: Crossway, 2001), 94.

3. Ibid., 95.

4. Meredith G. Kline, "Genesis," in *The New Bible Commentary*, eds. D. Guthrie and J. A. Motyer (Grand Rapids: Eerdmans, 1970), 88.

5. R. C. Sproul, ed., *New Geneva Study Bible* (Nashville: Thomas Nelson, 1995), 19.

6. John M. Frame, *No Other God: A Response to Open Theism* (Phillipsburg, N.J.: Presbyterian and Reformed, 2001), 176.

7. John H. Sailhamer, "Genesis," in vol. 2 of *The Expositor's Bible Commentary*, ed. Frank E. Gaebelein (Grand Rapids: Zondervan, 1990), 80–81.

8. Meredith G. Kline, *Kingdom Prologue* (Overland Park, Kans.: Two Age Press, 2000), 216.

9. Sailhamer, *Genesis*, 80.

Noah Built an Ark

Genesis 6:9–16

9 *This is the account of Noah.*

Noah was a righteous man, blameless among the people of his time, and he walked with God. **10** *Noah had three sons: Shem, Ham and Japheth.*

11 *Now the earth was corrupt in God's sight and was full of violence.* **12** *God saw how corrupt the earth had become, for all the people on earth had corrupted their ways.* **13** *So God said to Noah, "I am going to put an end to all people, for the earth is filled with violence because of them. I am surely going to destroy both them and the earth.* **14** *So make yourself an ark of cypress wood; make rooms in it and coat it with pitch inside and out.* **15** *This is how you are to build it: The ark is to be 450 feet long, 75 feet wide and 45 feet high.* **16** *Make a roof for it and finish the ark to within 18 inches of the top. Put a door in the side of the ark and make lower, middle and upper decks.*

AFTER HAVING studied the generations from Adam's line, we now come to a new section on the life of Noah introduced by, "This is the account of Noah." It is not an account of his descendants, which comes in chapters 10 and 11, but of events in his lifetime. The Flood narrative actually begins with verses 5–12 where we are told of God's decision to send the Flood because of people's wickedness, particularly for their violence against the righteous. But within God's plan, he intended to rescue Noah and his household.

The Flood is of great significance as a time of judgment on humanity between the Creation-Fall events and the end of the age. In the New Testament, the Flood is given universal significance for its symbolism in salvation and judgment as well as in marking the end of one epoch and beginning another in God's plan for people's redemption. In the transition between the two epochs, God instructed Noah to make a microcosmic floating house typifying the heavenly sanctuary.

∾ Noah Walked with God

"Noah was a righteous man, blameless among the people of his time, and he walked with God" (Gen. 6:9). Repeatedly, the Scriptures tell us that Noah was exceptionally righteous (Gen. 7:1; Ezek. 14:14, 20; Heb. 11:7; 2 Pet. 2:5). Some see in this an explanation as to why Noah found favor or grace with God (v. 8). (See in chapter 4 the relevance of this for the interpretation of Noah as covenant grantee being a type of Christ.) Of course, the LORD was pleased with Noah's blameless life. However, readers should carefully note the order and literary structure of Genesis 6:8 and 9. Verse 8 is the last verse of the book of Adam, and verse 9 is the first verse of the book of Noah. Ten such divisions are within the Book of Genesis, each beginning a major section. The end of the book of Adam told us that God's favor came on Noah after a description of humanity's depravity. Then the beginning of the book of Noah informed us that he was a man of integrity. No explanation was given in verse 8 as to why God favored Noah in the midst of a humanity whose thoughts were continually evil. It was simply a matter of God's choice (Rom. 9:15, 16). Nothing in Noah caused God to favor him, but God's grace came to him simply due to God's particularity in his redemptive plan. The nature of God's grace is that he gives it to those who do not deserve it. In this case, God's grace was expressed in extreme particularity in that it focused on one person, Noah, and because of him, included his family. The result of Noah receiving God's favor was that he became righteous and came into a relationship with God (v. 9). God's grace reigns through righteousness (Rom. 5:21) so that through God's grace we become righteous. We cannot be righteous before our holy God in a fallen world through our own efforts. Since we are all born in sin in rebellion against God, we cannot initiate righteousness in order to obtain grace.[1] This grace displayed toward Noah is an early expression of a repeated theme in the covenant of redemption.

Noah's name has a similar sound to the Hebrew word for *comfort,* for he was to bring comfort to humankind from the grief and pain caused by their rebellion (Gen. 5:29). He would also bring comfort to God, whose heart was grieved over people's every inclination toward evil. Of course, this does not mean that Noah was without sin (cf. Gen. 9:21). He was part of the fallen race that had broken the creational covenant of works made with Adam. Noah was the recipient of God's sovereign grace through an act of pure mercy in Christ. Grace is *hen* (חֵן) in Hebrew, which is a reversal of the consonants of Noah's name, forming a wordplay on the name. Additionally, Noah's name reflects the Sabbath ordinance. Lamech named his son Noah, which besides being translated "comfort" also meant "rest" or "quiet" from "the labor and painful toil of our hands" (Gen. 5:29). The word for *rest* is not the same used for *Sabbath,* but the concept is the same. We will rest from the work, that brings grief and sorrow to our souls, because we now rest through the work of God in us. The "painful toil of our hands" is the labor and misery we endure by the sweat of our brow in working the cursed ground (Gen. 3:17–19). Noah would bring rest from the trouble, wickedness, and sin in the world. Lamech intended to establish "a standing monument of his own wishes and hopes,"[2] looking forward to the promised Redeemer. The comfort from our sinful works in the flesh is found in the remission of them by the work of the Messiah and in the purging of them by the Spirit in our sanctification. Thus, we are comforted from the miseries of this life by delighting in God's goodness and enjoying his love. We receive some preludes of relief from the curse on the ground now, but we chiefly look forward to the freedom our souls will have from bodies that will return to dust and eternal glorified bodies living in many rooms (as in the palace of a king) prepared for us (John 14:2). This blessed hope is what Lamech looked forward to in the naming of Noah.

Despite being a sinner like the rest of humanity, Noah was a man of integrity. It is hard to find a person like that today. How much more so in Noah's day when everyone around him was corrupt and violent. It is difficult to stand alone when everyone else compromises God's standards. The world ridicules those persons who are the only ones to take a righteous stand. The reason Noah lived a righteous life was because "he walked with God." Enoch is the only other person so described in the Scriptures. An intentional parallel is made between them to show that as Noah was delivered from the Flood, Enoch was delivered from suffering death. God made clear that he will deliver those who walk with God and do not corrupt their ways.

Noah had an intimate communion with his Maker. Peter commended him as "a preacher of righteousness" (2 Pet. 2:5). God gave Noah repeated special revelations before the Flood, as it began, when it ended, and afterward. Revelation as the Flood began was particularly noted in that "the LORD shut him in" (Gen. 7:16) the ark just before the rain started. Noah heard God's voice and obeyed him. He believed what the LORD said and acted on it, so God protected him from judgment. In Noah we see a type of Jesus who always did what pleased his Father (John 8:29).

How can we hear God's voice today? We don't have new special revelations, but we do have God's completed special revelation, the Bible, the Word of God. In the Word we find Jesus, who came as the Word incarnate. As we hear the Word preached, taught, and modeled by others, and as we read, study, memorize, meditate on, and pray through the Word, we will hear God's voice and walk with him. Let us obey what we hear God saying through his Word, and we too will be righteous for soon we will reflect God's character and values in our own lives.

As "a preacher of righteousness," Noah warned the ungodly of the coming judgment through a flood. This was evidence of his great faith in God's word. Perhaps his building activity on the ark was his primary means of preaching righteousness. "With every day of construction he proclaimed the judgment of God against sin and the grace of God in offering deliverance."[3] But certainly he must have also verbalized his message of warning, calling for repentance. He was a prophetic witness to his generation of the need to repent from corruption and violence and to live righteously before a holy God. This is what Jesus did as well (Matt. 11:20–24; 23:1–36). Again we see that Noah was a type of Christ in his role as a prophet, in his walk with God, and in his doing the will of God.

What we need today are more people like Noah who will take a stand for the Lord as righteous, blameless people, witnessing to the power of God for our salvation. Will we be among them?

God Avenges the Death of His Faithful Remnant

God destroyed the world because "the earth was corrupt in [His] sight and was full of violence. . . . So God said to Noah, 'I am going to put an end to all people, for the earth is filled with violence

because of them'" (Gen. 6:11, 13). This violence began with unbe-
lieving Cain's murder of his righteous brother Abel. The LORD said
to Cain, "Your brother's blood cries out to me from the ground"
(Gen. 4:10). Isaiah made a clear allusion to Genesis 7:16 when he
spoke to Judah, celebrating the resurrection of the righteous and
the protection of God's remnant people from his wrath against the
world. In death they are protected behind shut doors. God asserts
that he will bring justice for the violence done against them.

> See, the LORD is coming out of his dwelling
>> to punish the people of the earth for their sins.
> The earth will disclose the blood shed upon her;
>> she will conceal her slain no longer. (Isa. 26:21)

This is what finally happened on the day of the Flood. The oppressive
powers who had killed the righteous would no longer go unpunished.
The blood of the godly cried out to God against their murderers. It
was time for God's justice to avenge their deaths. In fact, this was a
cause for praise to God. David sang such praise saying,

> Sing praises to the LORD, enthroned in Zion;
>> proclaim among the nations what he has done.
> For he who avenges blood remembers;
>> he does not ignore the cry of the afflicted. (Ps. 9:11, 12)

God still holds accountable the murderers of his martyrs. Jesus
warned the teachers of the Law and the Pharisees saying that all the
righteous blood shed on earth, from Abel to Zechariah (the whole
Old Testament), would come on that generation. How would they
"escape being condemned to hell"? (Matt. 23:33–36). By persecut-
ing Christ, they were identified with their murderous ancestors.
God's judgment came with the destruction of the Temple and
Jerusalem in AD 70. Yet the ultimate judgment for the blood of the

martyrs will come at the end of the age. When the Lamb opened the fifth seal in John's vision in Revelation, the souls of those who had been killed "because of the word of God and the testimony they had maintained" called out loudly, "How long, Sovereign Lord, holy and true, until you judge the inhabitants of the earth and avenge our blood?" (Rev. 6:9, 10). In the spiritual battle at the end of the age, the great prostitute Babylon will be defeated, and a great multitude in heaven will shout,

"Hallelujah!
Salvation and glory and power belong to our God,
for true and just are his judgments.
He has condemned the great prostitute
who corrupted the earth by her adulteries.
He has avenged on her the blood of his servants." (Rev. 19:1, 2)

Jesus will ultimately bring judgment on the earth (John 5:22) to avenge the martyrdom of his saints. In our day we have more martyrs for faith in Jesus Christ than at any other period in world history. Currently, there are about 166,000 martyrs per year.[4] As I write this, more than ten thousand Christians have just been killed in central Nigerian villages by Muslim extremists with external mercenaries. No worldwide outcry was made to this news because it was kept quiet for political reasons.

∽ God Designed an Ark

No sooner had God pronounced judgment on all humanity and the earth than he also provided a plan for the salvation of the righteous. God gave Noah every detail for the construction of an ark to save his household and the animals. The Hebrew word for *ark*, an Egyptian loan word, means "chest" or "box," when applied to the ark of the covenant (Exod. 25:10; Num. 3:31). Our English word *ark* comes from the Latin Vulgate translation *arca* meaning "box." The only other place the Hebrew word for ark is used in the Bible is in Exodus (2:3, 5) in reference to the basket in which baby Moses was placed. Both were covered with pitch to make them watertight. Both were used to deliver those in them from death. The ark actually was a seaworthy house. The author seems to specifically avoid using the term for ship.

The dimensions of the ark were about 450 by 75 by 45 feet (Gen. 6:15),[5] similar in size to a large battleship or a small cargo ship. It would have been two and a half times as big as the large ancient Egyptian wooden cargo ships during the Early Dynastic Period (1550–1400 BC), which measured up to 170 feet long. Archeologists have found that evidence from earliest Near Eastern civilization indicates that there was sufficient skill in architectural design and woodworking to build such a structure. Its dimensions were ideal for a safe and seaworthy craft. Its large dimensions to accommodate the representative animals and people for a year reflect "how wide and long and high and deep is the love of Christ" (Eph. 3:18) to save his elect for eternity.

The ark was designed for floating like a barge, but it had no rudder or sail. Its destination was completely in the hands of the LORD. This is also true of our salvation. "Salvation comes from the LORD" (Jon. 2:9). Our destination is entered by faith.

The ark's design came completely from the LORD, for no person could have conceived of such a vessel without a knowledge of something similar. Its design was by supernatural revelation. With great faith, Noah believed the word of the LORD and built the ark, even though he had never seen one (Heb. 11:7). He also had possibly never seen rain or a flood, for up to that time a mist went up from the ground and watered the earth (Gen. 2:6). By faith, in holy fear of God's warning, Noah spent 120 years building an ark of 43,300 tons displacement[6] to save himself, his family, and the animals.

Just as Noah by faith built the ark and was saved, even though he had never seen a ship, rain, or a flood, so too we must believe God's

Word to be saved. We have never seen the resurrected Christ, but we believe in him because we believe God's Word as found in the Holy Scriptures. Noah was saved just as we are, by faith in the promised Redeemer, Jesus Christ, who is the eternal Word of God (John 1:1, 2). Noah's life, ministry, and deliverance were a type of our salvation in Christ.

It is interesting to note a similarity in the accounts of God's creation (Gen. 1), the building of the ark, and the building of the Tabernacle (Exod. 25ff.). A similar pattern may be seen in that God commanded an action, and the command was carried out according to his will. Each narrative ends with God's blessing. In both the making of the ark and the making of the Tabernacle, God established a covenant. Although not mentioned explicitly in Genesis 1—3, later biblical tradition associated a covenant made with Adam (Hosea 6:7). The elements of a covenant were also present in the Garden of Eden. God gave detailed specifications for building the ark, as in building the Tabernacle, and they were recorded for us not so much that we might know the details of what they looked like "but rather that we might appreciate the meticulous care with which these godly and exemplary men went about their tasks of obedience to God's will. They obeyed God with 'all their hearts.' "[7]

The design of the ark had a more profound meaning in that it represented the kingdom of God as a capsulated city of God. It was a perfect cultural-urban structure that typified the house of God. It has similarities to the Creator's cosmic house of heaven and earth typified in Israel's Tabernacle and Temple. The architectural features of the ark were more like a house than a sailing vessel with its three stories, the window, and the door. The three stories correspond to the three stories of the world envisioned in the heavens above, the earth beneath, and the realm under the earth, particularly associated with the waters (cf. Exod. 20:4; Deut. 4:17, 18). It is possible that the three zones were reinforced by the animal lists of "every kind of bird, of every kind of animal and of every kind of creature that moves along the ground" (Gen. 6:20; cf. 6:7; 7:14, 21, 23; 8:17, 19). The realm under the earth may be either the burrowing creatures or the fact that the lowest part of the ark was submerged underwater.

The pitch with which God instructed Noah to cover the ark both inside and out to prevent seepage of water is called *cophir* in Hebrew, which also means "expiation" and "a price of redemption." This is an excellent allusion to the expiation and redemption we have through the blood of Christ, which covers our sins and protects us "from the deluge of divine vengeance."[8]

The window of the ark, going completely around it (Gen. 6:16), has its counterpart in the window of heaven mentioned in this account as the "floodgates of the heavens" (7:11; 8:2). The door held back the chaotic waters. This imagery is seen in the LORD's response to Job out of the storm.

> "Who shut up the sea behind doors
> >   when it burst forth from the womb,
> when I made the clouds its garment
> >   and wrapped it in thick darkness,
> when I fixed limits for it
> >   and set its doors and bars in place,
> when I said, 'This far you may come and no farther;
> >   here is where your proud waves halt'?" (Job 38:8–11)

The window and door reflect the cosmic source of the floodwaters: the "floodgates of the heavens" and the "springs of the great deep" which burst forth (Gen. 7:11). One door in the ark reflects the one way to salvation through Christ and his kingdom. This is also reflected in the one entrance to the courtyard of the Tabernacle (Exod. 38:18).

The cosmic house symbolism is further confirmed in that God revealed its design, as mentioned above. Whenever God revealed an architectural plan in Scripture, it was for his sanctuary-house—the Tabernacle, the Temple, or the new Jerusalem (Exod. 25ff.; 1 Chron. 28:11–19; Heb. 9:1–5; cf. Ezek. 40ff.; Rev. 21:10–22). As the original Creator, who alone understands the universe (Job 38), only God could give humanity the plan for a microcosmic model of his sanctuary. We see that Abraham too looked "forward to the city with foundations, whose architect and builder is God" (Heb. 11:10). In light of this, we see that God is "providing plans for a symbolic, prophetic copy of that heavenly sanctuary, the final objective of man's cultural history."[9] When we ultimately enter that Holy City, we will not see a temple, "because the Lord God Almighty and the Lamb are its temple," and it will be filled with the glory of God (Rev. 21:22, 23).

SCRIPTURE READING:

PSALM 9

Discussion Questions

1. What is meant by "Noah was a righteous man" (Gen. 6:9)? Did God look with favor on Noah because he was righteous or because God was gracious?
2. What was the "comfort" or "rest" that Lamech looked forward to in naming his son Noah?
3. How does the righteousness of Noah relate to God commanding him to make an ark?
4. Why did God decide to destroy the earth? What comfort does this bring for today's martyrs?
5. What is significant about God's instructions on how the ark should be built?
6. In what sense is the ark a type of the kingdom of God entered through Jesus Christ?

Notes

1. J. Ligon Duncan III, "Covenant of Preservation—Noah," *Covenant Theology* (Jackson, Miss.: First Presbyterian Church, 2000), audiocassette.

2. Herman Witsius, *The Economy of the Covenants between God and Man*, vol. 2 (Reprint, Kingsburg, Calif.: den Dulk Christian Foundation, 1990), 130.

3. Howard F. Vos, *Genesis*, vol. 1 of *Everyman's Bible Commentary* (Chicago: Moody Press, 1982), 47.

4. David B. Barrett and Todd M. Johnson, "Annual Statistical Table on Global Mission: 2003," *International Bulletin of Missionary Research* 27, no. 1 (January 2003): 25.

5. This is assuming a cubit to equal 18 inches. However, in ancient times there were variations in the measurement of a cubit, which could be as long as 22 inches. Therefore, some assume an ark of 500 feet in length, four stories high.

6. Some commentators say 15,000 tons displacement.

7. John Sailhamer, "Genesis," in vol. 2 of *The Expositor's Bible Commentary*, ed. Frank E. Gaebelein (Grand Rapids: Zondervan, 1990), 82–83.

8. Witsius, *Economy of the Covenants*, 198, 199.

9. Meredith G. Kline, *Kingdom Prologue* (Overland Park, Kans.: Two Age Press, 2000), 225–227.

A Covenant of Redemptive Judgment

Genesis 6:17–22

17 *"I am going to bring floodwaters on the earth to destroy all life under the heavens, every creature that has the breath of life in it. Everything on earth will perish.*

*   **18** *But I will establish my covenant with you, and you will enter the ark—you and your sons and your wife and your sons' wives with you.* **19** *You are to bring into the ark two of all living creatures, male and female, to keep them alive with you.* **20** *Two of every kind of bird, of every kind of animal and of every kind of creature that moves along the ground will come to you to be kept alive.* **21** *You are to take every kind of food that is to be eaten and store it away as food for you and for them."*

*   **22** *Noah did everything just as God commanded him.*

A S THE LORD continued to speak to Noah, he made a drastic contrast between what he was going to do with the world and what he was going to do with Noah. The time for a judicial verdict and judgment had come for the world. The means by which the outcome of the trial would be determined was by judicial ordeal. The LORD knew the outcome, for it was all under his control. He made a solemn promise to Noah and his household to preserve them through the ordeal on condition that they obey his commands. Noah demonstrated his faith in God's word by doing everything God commanded. Noah then became a model for our own faith.

⁓ Trial by Judicial Ordeal

The author of Hebrews warned us, "It is a dreadful thing to fall into the hands of the living God" (Heb. 10:31). A prime example of this is illustrated in the Flood. God decided that he would settle the question of who would ultimately rule in the dispute between the kingdom of this world ruled by Satan and the kingdom of God by the procedure of judicial ordeal. This was a common form of ascertaining the judgment of the gods in the ancient world. It took a variety of forms, such as individual combat between adversaries or trial by passing through water or fire. A divine verdict was determined by whether the person survived the ordeal or not. Some ordeals served to both determine guilt and to execute the guilty. The Deluge was the classic example of one variety, the river ordeal.

The Flood was not the only trial by ordeal in Scripture, but it is found numerous places. God used a judicial ordeal in delivering Israel out of Egypt by using both the water of the Red Sea and fire from the glory cloud. As in the Flood, the ordeal served the dual purpose of both vindication-deliverance for Israel and condemnation-destruction for the Egyptians. Water and fire blended in Daniel's vision of a river of fire flowing from God's throne (Dan. 7:10). Psalm 66 speaks of how God tested and refined his people like silver (v. 10). "You let men ride over our heads; we went through fire and water, but you brought us to a place of abundance" (Ps. 66:12). Isaiah prophesied deliverance for God's people when they "pass through the waters" and "walk through the fire" (Isa. 43:2). Peter told us that at the end of the age a fire ordeal will be used to bring judgment on the wicked and vindication for the righteous (2 Pet. 3:7). Peter and Paul identified the Deluge and the Exodus as baptismal events (1 Cor. 10:1, 2; 1 Pet. 3:20, 21). Consequently, we understand baptismal waters as a passage through the ordeal of death.

Noah was delivered through the water ordeal by his faith. "By faith Noah, when warned about things not yet seen, in holy fear built an ark to save his family. By his faith he condemned the world and became heir of the righteousness that comes by faith" (Heb. 11:7). The Deluge ordeal condemned and destroyed the claims on the world made by the wicked and justly punished their sins. However, Noah and his household emerged victorious through the ordeal with a verdict in their favor.

Their passing through the waters of death to life is identified with the resurrection of Jesus Christ (1 Pet. 3:20, 21). Because of their faith, they were justified, having inherited the righteousness of Christ, and they were given the kingdom of God.[1] Similarly, the coming judgment at the end of the age will be for our salvation. Through it we will emerge victorious in our resurrection, and the world will be renewed with the consummation of the kingdom of God.

∾ God Established a Covenant

The LORD told Noah, "Everything on earth will perish. But I will establish my covenant with you, and you will enter the ark—you and your sons and your wife and your sons' wives with you" (Gen. 6:18).

A covenant established by God is a unilateral agreement that binds people in a defined relationship with him according to his promise. God made promises to people with whom he established special relationships. A covenant assures a believer of the certainty of God's promises to him or her. God established his covenant of grace with his chosen people by promising them a Savior.

Notice that God took the initiative to establish his covenant with Noah. However, Noah's responsibility was to respond to God's favor by obeying him. His obedience did not purchase God's favor. It was not obedience that led God to notice Noah in the first place.[2] However, as the recipient of a covenant of grant, Noah was rewarded for his obedience made possible through his walk with God.

The LORD was not referring to his future covenant of common grace toward all creatures that he would make of never destroying the earth again by flood (9:9–11). God seemed to be confirming a past covenant already existing because the Hebrew language (*hakim berith*) does not denote the initiation of a new covenant. This is the first place the Hebrew term *berith* (בְּרִית, "covenant") occurs in Genesis, but the concept and related terms were already found in earlier chapters. God's covenant confirmed an already existing relationship. It formalized and gave concrete expression to preserve this relationship. Because Noah was the particular person remembered (8:1) in the salvation event fulfilling this covenant, it meant that the covenant was specifically made with him rather than with all creation. God assured Noah that he would fulfill his promise of salvation. It declared his intention, while the LORD's remembering (8:1) was the fulfilling of that intention.

But what Noah and his household went through in the ark was not the ultimate fulfillment of their salvation but just a typological sign of entrance to the kingdom of God. The patriarchs in Seth's line had waited in faith for the fulfillment of God's covenant promises. They would not finally see them fulfilled until the day of judgment when the elect would inherit the kingdom of God. However, it was fulfilled in type with the covenant established with Noah.

The literary structure of the Flood episode confirms the thought that the covenant of Genesis 6:18 was a covenant of salvation, different from the common-grace covenant of 8:21–9:17 made with all the earth. The covenant of 6:18 was fulfilled within the historical period of the Flood and its abatement. It was made only with the holy covenant community, promising them the kingdom of salvation. God's remembrance of Noah (8:1) as the ark was about to rest confirmed the fulfillment of the promise made to him.

Because God delivered Noah through the ordeal of judgment and later promised him preservation from flood again, Palmer Robertson calls it a "covenant of preservation." He defines God's covenants with humankind as a "bond-in-blood sovereignly administered." The sense in which the covenant with Noah was a bond-in-blood may be seen in the major underlying motifs of life and death. Noah, carrying the Seed of the woman, found grace in the eyes of the LORD and was given life through the judgment. The rest of humanity, apart from his covenant family, was destroyed in the ordeal of judgment, for they were of the seed of Satan. God established capital punishment for the one who takes another's life (Gen. 9:6). Thus, life and death are found here with preservation for the one who keeps the stipulations of the covenant and death for the covenant breaker. Robertson does not distinguish between the antediluvian covenant mentioned in Genesis 6:18 with that of the postdiluvian covenant in 8:21–9:17. He divides the nature of the covenant with Noah into four sections—Genesis 6:17–22; 8:20–22; 9:1–7; 9:8–17—all relating to a commitment to preserve Noah and his family. He sees the preservation of Noah through the Flood as integral to the "preservation" principle seen in the covenant after the Flood.[3]

Although the connection between the antediluvian covenant and postdiluvian covenant with Noah has a common theme of preservation, I agree with Meredith Kline in seeing the two as distinctive covenants. The covenant mentioned in Genesis 6:18 refers to the relationship between God and Noah, while the covenant in Genesis 9:8–17 is with Noah, his offspring, every living creature, and the earth. Within the antediluvian covenant we find themes of both judgment and salvation. Rather than the covenant being confirmed by oath with symbolic judgment, such as when God made his covenant with Abram by means of the smoking firepot going between the split-apart animals (Gen. 15:17–21), this covenant was confirmed by actual deliverance through a real divine judgment.[4] In the same way, Jesus established the new covenant in his blood by taking our deserved judgment on himself by dying on the cross.

A Baptismal Covenant

God established his covenant not just with Noah but also with Noah's wife, his three sons, and their wives. This was a repeated theme (Gen. 6:18; 7:1, 7, 13, 23; 8:16, 18; 9:9, 12). All of them were brought into the ark to be saved. But note that the covenant was made with Noah alone, "you" being singular in "I will establish my covenant with you" (6:18) and "I have found you righteous" (7:1). Because Noah as head of the household was righteous, his whole family entered the ark to be saved.

This is a consistent pattern of how God works through families (Gen. 17:7, 10, 12, 23; Acts 2:39; 1 Cor. 7:14). God often saves an entire family unit, including the children (Acts 16:15, 31–34; 1 Cor. 1:16). It illustrates the moral and responsible relationship that parents have over their children. For this reason, Hebrews tells us, "By faith Noah, when warned about things not yet seen, in holy fear built an ark to save his family" (Heb. 11:7).

In the context of the Flood account, covenant headship further illustrated the principle of the sign of the covenant, the Flood as a type of baptism, being given to the children of believing parents. This covenant with Noah and his household did not mean that all the household members were among the elect (cf. Gen. 9:22, 25).

Similarly, not all baptized children of believing parents, although they are within the covenant community, confess faith in Christ. Only at the consummation, at the end of the age when Jesus brings everyone under judicial scrutiny will the circle of the elect and the covenant community completely coincide (Matt. 13:24–30, 36–43). Until that time, we are called into covenant community in the church with parents bringing their children into the household of God. It is contrary to biblical principles for anyone to remain isolated as a Christian apart from the covenant family.

The deliverance of Noah and his family through the Flood was a type of our salvation through Jesus Christ. It illustrated how God redeems his children. As Peter wrote,

> "God waited patiently in the days of Noah while the ark was being built. In it only a few people, eight in all, were saved through water, and this water symbolizes baptism that now saves you also— not the removal of dirt from the body but the pledge of a good conscience toward God. It saves you by the resurrection of Jesus Christ." (1 Pet. 3:20, 21)

We have in this passage a double figure. The Flood symbolizes baptism, and baptism symbolizes salvation. Baptism is a sign of entering into a new covenant relationship with God. Through the Flood, a baptism of redemptive judgment, Noah and his family were saved. The ark symbolized God's kingdom in a cosmic spiritual house, which saves his elect from judgment when they enter it. The water of the Flood brought the death of those under judgment. The water of baptism symbolizes the death of Christ for us in taking our deserved judgment.

Water also symbolizes our death to our old way of life and identifies us with Christ in his death, burial, and resurrection (Rom. 6:3–5). So Peter said that we are saved by trusting in and identifying ourselves with Jesus Christ, just as Noah and his family trusted in God's promises of salvation from judgment by entering the ark. An appropriate hymn by Edward Mote reminds us in whom our trust must be.

> His oath, His covenant, His blood,
> Support me in the whelming flood;
> When all around my soul gives way,
> He then is all my hope and stay.
>
> On Christ, the solid Rock, I stand;
> All other ground is sinking sand.

The waters of judgment in the Flood also were purifying. Symbolically, they washed away the sins of the world. For most people they led to their condemnation, but for the elect family, they were the means of their salvation through the ark-kingdom. Water has a purifying effect as did the sprinkled blood of old (Ezek. 36:25; Heb. 9:13, 14, 19; 10:22; 1 Pet. 1:2). Through the blood of Christ, we are purified from all sin (1 John 1:7) for Christ took the judgment that we deserve.

Since the ark passing through the Flood symbolized Christ delivering us from God's judgment, it is interesting to note that God instructed Noah to build only one door to the ark without giving its dimension (Gen. 6:16). Only by going through that one door could Noah and his family be saved. Likewise, we can only be saved in one way—by faith in God's provision through Christ. The door was large enough for any sinner to enter. Jesus said, "I am the door. If anyone enters by me, he will be saved" (John 10:9 ESV). Today a large ship or building has several entrances and exits for safety. But all were safe in the ark, for God was with them. Just as "God was reconciling the world to himself in Christ" (2 Cor. 5:19), so the LORD was in the ark with Noah as a type of Christ within us. Since God was with

Noah, he was safe from judgment. Since God is with us, we too are safe from damnation.

∼ Noah as Covenant Grantee

Previously, we saw how the LORD was grieved that he had made people on the earth because of their great wickedness. "But Noah found favor in the eyes of the LORD" (Gen. 6:8). Additionally, "Noah was a righteous man, blameless among the people of his time" (6:9); "Noah did everything just as God commanded him" (6:22); and God said, "I have found you righteous in this generation" (7:1).

This is all relevant to the type of covenant God made with Noah. He was the recipient of a covenant of grant, the type given by a king to a servant for faithful, exceptional service. Normally, this meant granting the servant a special status by giving him title over cities or land with exemptions from normal obligations of revenue. The actual reward of God's covenant with Noah was realized through his directions for building and filling the ark, leading to his entering the kingdom of God and receiving salvation. Noah's receiving this covenant of grant was clearly due to his righteous behavior and walk with God. A clear contrast was made between him and the corruption and violence of the rest of the world. However, at another level, Noah's righteousness was due to the grace of God extended to him prior to this time. He was from Seth's believing covenantal family line. The covenant of Genesis 6:18 confirmed the relationship. "But Noah found favor [grace] in the eyes of the LORD" (Gen. 6:8). The meaning of this is not that Noah received this favor even though he was just like everybody else. No, he was different from them and so was deserving of favorable treatment. So God's grace toward Noah through the covenant was not just an act of mercy. Of course, since people are saved by the gospel through God's sovereign grace, this covenant of grant falls under the administration of the covenant of grace (Gen. 3:15). It is only through the power of God in freely offering his forgiving grace that anyone is brought into a right relationship with him. However, Noah found favor with the LORD and so received the covenant of grant for his loyal service to his Sovereign. Similar terms for recipients of royal grants were noted in ancient documents.

At the basic level of our relationship with God, salvation is a matter of sovereign grace. But God works with his people on two levels or spheres. At another typological level, God gives the rewards of the kingdom to believers on the basis of their obedient performance of covenantal duty. At this level, it is a typological representation of the Messiah and his kingdom. On occasion, God used certain individuals with exemplary behavior to become typological signs of the Messiah's obedience to secure the kingdom of God for himself and his loyal servants. Abraham, Phinehas, and David were recipients of similar covenantal grants as rewards for their faithfulness. Their outstanding faithful service was given typological significance. In this way, they pointed to Christ as the one who fulfilled a covenant of works by living a sinless life, which had been failed by Adam, and who "received the grant of the kingdom for the obedient fulfillment of his covenantal mission."[5]

A common theme of all those who received the covenant of grant for meritorious service was victory in the holy war against Satan and his earthly followers. Before receiving his covenant grant, Abraham defeated the five kings of the East (Gen. 14). Phinehas threw a spear through an adulterous couple, which stopped the plague from killing all the Israelites who were led into idolatry by the Moabites and Midianites (Num. 25). David defeated the Philistines, captured Jerusalem from the Jebusites, and brought the Tabernacle to the city of David prior to receiving his covenant grant (2 Sam. 5–7). From the context of Genesis 6:1–13, we may presume that God also rewarded Noah for his courageous prophetic stand against apostasy and the corrupt and violent world rulers of his day.

We need to look at this works-grant to Noah as a type of the kingdom secured through his righteousness. Remembering this to be a type, we have no conflict with the fundamental level of God saving his people only by grace. The judgment seen in the Flood was a type of the last judgment to be overseen by the Messiah. The kingdom granted to Noah in the ark was only a type of the messianic kingdom to be consummated when Christ returns. The covenant of grant given to Noah for his righteousness serves as a revelation of the gospel, for in that typological situation, Noah prefigured the Messiah. As Jesus lived a sinless and righteous life, the Father rewarded him with exalted glory and an eternal kingdom.

This provides the foundation for God extending his grace to his elect. As a type of Christ, Noah received a covenant of grant for his good works, just as the principle of works is the basis for God's redemptive grace through Christ. This is seen in that "through the obedience of the one man the many will be made righteous" (Rom. 5:19). This one man, Jesus Christ, found favor in the Father's eyes because of his perfect righteousness. On this basis, Christ's righteousness is applied to believers by grace through faith, which is a gift of God (Eph. 2:8). "Just as sin reigned in death, so also grace might reign through righteousness to bring eternal life through Jesus Christ our Lord" (Rom. 5:21).

Since Noah was a righteous servant as a type of Christ, he was a guaranty of his household's blessing and salvation. But aside from the typological representation of Noah for Christ, there naturally can be no comparison between them as to their actual righteousness. A similar comparison may be made with Israel's covenantal obedience and staying in the Promised Land despite the imperfections of individuals and the nation. However, when Israel acted wickedly, God removed them from the Promised Land, for they no longer maintained the type of the righteous in the eternal kingdom.

So in a general sense, Noah's righteousness was significant enough as an example to point to the perfect righteousness of the Messiah.

As Noah also was a surety of his household's salvation, so Christ is our surety of the fulfillment of God's promises in the new covenant. As Noah was the prophet-mediator of the covenant of grant to his household church, he typified Christ who inaugurated a new covenant as its Prophet-Mediator.

Finally, Noah prefigured Christ as the Savior-King, the one who delivers from judgment, defeats satanic forces, and builds the sanctuary-house of God. Noah "in holy fear built an ark to save his family" (Heb. 11:7). This act combined the elements of being the means of salvation from judgment, bringing liberation from the oppression of the serpent's seed, and building the symbolic cosmic house of God, a type of the consummated kingdom and goal of the covenant.[6]

☙ Noah Obeyed

Let us now look at Noah's obedience in a nontypological sense. "Noah did everything just as God commanded him" (Gen. 6:22). This is what it meant for Noah to "walk with God." It was a matter of "simple obedience to God's commands and trust in his provision."[7] Apparently, Noah loved God. John told us, "This is love for God: to obey his commands" (1 John 5:3). Although we may do 90 percent of what we are told to do, to not do it all is complete disobedience. True obedience is to do all that is required of us. This is what Noah did out of his love for God.

John continued, "And his commands are not burdensome, for everyone born of God overcomes the world. This is the victory that has overcome the world, even our faith" (1 John 5:3, 4). Noah's obedience was a sign of his faith. Through his faith, he condemned the world and had victory over it. Faith is not just believing in a theoretical sense but acting on what we believe. It is taking God at his word. Hebrews describes Noah's faith.

"By faith Noah, when warned about things not yet seen, in holy fear built an ark to save his family. By his faith he condemned the world and became heir of the righteousness that comes by faith." (Heb. 11:7)

Noah showed himself to be such a man of faith that he and his family were saved from the Flood. They did not suffer the judgment of the rest of the world. Noah condemned the world, recognizing the sinfulness of their way of living. God judged the world for their unbelief. By faith Noah believed what God said "when warned about things not yet seen."

The essence of faith is "being sure of what we hope for and certain of what we do not see" (Heb. 11:1). Noah showed his faith by building a huge ark on dry ground far from a great body of water. It was inconceivable that such an overwhelmingly large vessel would ever float in that landlocked region. When the Flood came, God's word to Noah proved to be true, and Noah's faith was vindicated. By acting on his faith in building the ark, he inherited eternal life. He "became heir of the righteousness that comes by faith" (Heb. 11:7). We must become righteous to enter eternal life. That righteousness is a gift from God and is mediated through Jesus Christ. The righteousness of Christ becomes our righteousness. Thus, God gladly receives us as his adopted children, and we reign with Christ for eternity.

The object of Noah's faith was Jesus Christ, although Noah only knew him as the promised Seed that would crush the serpent's head (Gen. 3:15) and through the types of his salvation seen in God's deliverance through the Deluge and in the altar sacrifices. But all these were just shadows of the reality to be completed in Christ (Heb. 10:1) when "the fulfillment of the ages has come" (1 Cor. 10:11).

The way Noah's faith was vindicated shows us that no matter what comes our way—deprivation, persecution, or loss—we must persevere in our faith. Noah faced the loss of his home, his land (he was a farmer, Gen. 9:20), and his friends. Surely, he was persecuted and ridiculed for his faith. As Paul said, "In fact, everyone who wants to live a godly life in Christ Jesus will be persecuted, while evil men and impostors will go from bad to worse, deceiving and being deceived" (2 Tim. 3:12, 13). Noah was part of the "great cloud of witnesses" who encourage us to "run with perseverance the race marked out for us." Noah had fixed his "eyes on Jesus, the author and perfector of our faith" (Heb. 12:1, 2). We have this encouragement from the Lord in Hebrews:

> So do not throw away your confidence; it will be richly rewarded. You need to persevere so that when you have done the will of God, you will receive what he has promised. For in just a very little while,
>
> > "He who is coming will come and will not delay.
> > But my righteous one will live by faith.
> > And if he shrinks back,
> > I will not be pleased with him."
>
> But we are not of those who shrink back and are destroyed, but of those who believe and are saved. (Heb. 10:35–39)

By faith we believe God's Word that he will come again, destroy the earth by fire, condemn those without faith, renew the heavens and earth, and redeem his faithful children.

Will we now live in the light of that knowledge? Will we in faith wait patiently for the Lord's salvation? Although we can't see Jesus Christ, we know from God's Word who he is, what he has done for our salvation, and that he will soon return for us while bringing unbelievers under his judgment. Our faith, which is more precious than gold, will be proved genuine when Jesus Christ is revealed to us. As Peter said, "Though you have not seen him, you love him; and even though you do not see him now, you believe in him and are filled with an inexpressible and glorious joy" (1 Pet. 1:8). That joy is because we are receiving salvation. We receive salvation by believing God's Word, which tells us of his Son, and acting on what we know to be true. That isn't any different than it was for Noah. He believed God's Word and acted on it. When we believe what God tells us of coming judgment and salvation from our sins, which is only through the one door into the ark of God's kingdom and sanctuary, we know we have entered into eternal life.

SCRIPTURE READING:
Psalm 29

Discussion Questions

1. What type do we see in the judgment ordeal by water that has reference to our salvation?
2. What is the significance of the covenant God made with Noah?
3. Is it proper to speak of one or two covenants with Noah? If two, how were they distinct from one another?
4. What is the relationship between Noah and his family's salvation through the Flood and our baptism and salvation?
5. What is a covenant of grant? How does this reveal Noah as a type of Christ?
6. Why is it significant that Noah obeyed the Lord in everything?
7. How was Noah saved?
8. How is Noah's faith an example for us?

Notes

1. Meredith G. Kline, *Kingdom Prologue* (Overland Park, Kans.: Two Age Press, 2000), 216–217.

2. J. Ligon Duncan III, "Covenant of Perservation—Noah," *Covenant Theology* (Jackson, Miss.: First Presbyterian Church, 2000), audiocassette.

3. O. Palmer Robertson, *The Christ of the Covenants* (Phillipsburg, N.J.: Presbyterian and Reformed, 1980), 109–110, 124.

4. Meredith G. Kline, "Genesis," in *The New Bible Commentary*, eds. D. Guthrie and J. A. Motyer (Grand Rapids: Eerdmans, 1970), 88.

5. Kline, *Kingdom Prologue*, 238.

6. This section is largely a summary of Meredith G. Kline's teaching in *Kingdom Prologue,* 234–241.

7. John Sailhamer, "Genesis" in vol. 2 of *The Expositor's Bible Commentary*, ed. Frank E. Gaebelein (Grand Rapids: Zondervan, 1990), 81.

The LORD
Shut the Door

Genesis 7:1–16

1 *The* LORD *then said to Noah, "Go into the ark, you and your whole family, because I have found you righteous in this generation.* **2** *Take with you seven of every kind of clean animal, a male and its mate, and two of every kind of unclean animal, a male and its mate,* **3** *and also seven of every kind of bird, male and female, to keep their various kinds alive throughout the earth.* **4** *Seven days from now I will send rain on the earth for forty days and forty nights, and I will wipe from the face of the earth every living creature I have made."*
5 *And Noah did all that the* LORD *commanded him.*

    6 *Noah was six hundred years old when the floodwaters came on the earth.* **7** *And Noah and his sons and his wife and his sons' wives entered the ark to escape the waters of the flood.* **8** *Pairs of clean and unclean animals, of birds and of all creatures that move along the ground,* **9** *male and female, came*

to Noah and entered the ark, as God had commanded Noah.
10 And after the seven days the floodwaters came on the earth.
11 In the six hundredth year of Noah's life, on the seventeenth
day of the second month—on that day all the springs of the great
deep burst forth, and the floodgates of the heavens were opened.
12 And rain fell on the earth forty days and forty nights.

13 On that very day Noah and his sons, Shem, Ham and
Japheth, together with his wife and the wives of his three sons,
entered the ark. 14 They had with them every wild animal
according to its kind, all livestock according to their kinds,
every creature that moves along the ground according to its
kind and every bird according to its kind, everything with
wings. 15 Pairs of all creatures that have the breath of life in
them came to Noah and entered the ark. 16 The animals
going in were male and female of every living thing, as God
had commanded Noah. Then the LORD shut him in.

WE SEE IN this account of Noah, his family, and the animals entering the ark a picture of the grace of God for our salvation. On the other hand, in the coming Flood we see the judgment of God toward the unrepentant. The LORD graciously shut Noah and his family in the ark to preserve them from death, but in being closed in, they had a representative death that protected them from judgment. The LORD thus fulfilled his covenant of preservation and redemption. As the rain poured down for forty days and nights, we see a frequently repeated illustration of a critical period of testing and sanctification in the history of redemption.

∾ Noah: Righteous and Obedient

"The LORD then said to Noah, 'Go into the ark, you and your whole family, because I have found you righteous in this generation' " (Gen. 7:1).

This was the last time the LORD spoke to Noah prior to the Flood. Noah gave evidence of his deep faith by his actions, for he obeyed the LORD. He and his family, eight in all, went into the ark. Despite the ridicule and rejection of all the other people on the earth to heed his warning of the coming judgment, Noah obeyed. Thus, we are told, "And Noah did all that the LORD commanded him" (v. 5).

Through repetition, Moses made his message clear. Four times we are told that those who survived the Flood did all that God commanded (6:22; 7:5, 9, 16). The point is that obedience to the LORD is the way of salvation. This theme of obedience is repeated later concerning Abraham (Gen. 12:4; 21:4) and then the Israelites (Exod. 12:28). Obedience is a demonstration of true faith. As Hebrews tells us, "By faith Noah, when warned about things not yet seen, in holy fear built an ark to save his family." That was in obedience to the LORD's command. "By his faith he condemned the world and became heir of the righteousness that comes by faith" (Heb. 11:7). So it was through Noah's faith that he became righteous in God's sight. He had faith in the LORD's provision for his salvation. That provision is seen in the saving work of Jesus Christ, which was typified by the ark passing through the Deluge.

The LORD found Noah "righteous in this generation" (Gen. 7:1). This was not because of anything inherent in Noah himself, who was clearly a sinner like the rest of us (Gen. 8:21; 9:20). Beauty is in the eye of the beholder. A small child may feel a ragged, dirty doll is her most precious possession because it does something for her heart affection. Similarly, we have nothing lovely in ourselves, but God sees us as precious to him. He sees us through the righteousness of Jesus Christ who made us righteous and holy (1 Cor. 1:30). That is what God sees in us who believe and what he saw in Noah.

God's choice of Noah to be saved and his family's salvation because of him demonstrates an extreme narrowing of God's electing grace out of the millions who were passed over and justly left to die in their sins. This can only be understood in the light of the horrendous offense of our sins to God's holy character. It addresses questions as to the justice and fairness of God. This is why Moses makes so much of the sins of humanity at the end of the account of Adam and in the beginning of the account of Noah. To delve into the decrees of God and predestination at this point is to get sidetracked from the main issue of our sins deserving God's wrath. As those who have received the grace of God, this makes us appreciate our salvation all the more.

The saving of Noah and his family was a prototype of the salvation the LORD gives to his entire elect remnant. The day the Flood came is similar to the coming of the Day of the Lord, Jesus' Second Coming, when the righteous and the wicked are separated. John the Baptist described Jesus' future ministry like this: " 'His winnowing fork is in his hand, and he will clear his threshing floor, gathering his wheat into the barn and burning up the chaff with unquenchable fire' " (Matt. 3:12). When a farmer separates wheat from chaff and straw, he may use a winnowing fork to throw the grain up in the air as the wind blows the chaff away from the grain. Thus, the grain falls to the ground at the farmer's feet. Then he gathers the grain to be stored in the barn, but the chaff is refuse and is burned. Similarly in this imagery, believers will be separated from unbelievers at the last day.

"And Noah and his sons and his wife and his sons' wives entered the ark to escape the waters of the flood" (Gen. 7:7). Entering the ark took a tremendous act of faith. It became the grounds for Noah's condemning the world (Heb. 11:7). The worldly people refused to look to God's provision for salvation. The same condemnation is on those today who refuse to look on the Son of Man sent by God out of his love. "For God did not send his Son into the world to condemn the world, but to save the world through him. Whoever believes in him is not condemned, but whoever does not believe stands condemned already because he has not believed in the name of God's one and only Son" (John 3:17, 18).

On the seventeenth day of the second month of Noah's six hundredth year, the floodwaters burst forth. "On that very day," Noah and his family entered the ark. This phrase suggests a memorable occasion, as when Abraham and his household were circumcised (Gen. 17:23, 26), Israel came out of Egypt (Exod. 12:41, 51), and Moses went up Mount Nebo to view the Promised Land and die (Deut. 32:48). It indicated for Noah and his household that they were obedient to the LORD's command through their faith. It was their crossing of the Rubicon. There was no turning back. Through faith they had triumphed gloriously. They were now to enter a new beginning.

∼ Pairs of Animals Entered the Ark

"Pairs of clean and unclean animals, of birds and of all creatures that move along the ground, male and female, came to Noah and entered the ark, as God had commanded Noah" (Gen. 7:8, 9). The emphasis of this first section of chapter 7 is on seven pairs of clean animals entering the ark. Clean animals could be eaten or offered as sacrifices to God. The LORD gave Moses laws concerning what were considered clean animals. The ability to distinguish between clean and unclean animals must have already been given by divine revelation to Noah. However, Abel offered a clean animal, the firstborn of his flock, as a pleasing sacrifice to the LORD. So this distinction may have been known since the time of Adam when God covered Adam and Eve with animal skins, indicating sacrificed animals.

In Genesis 6, we saw parallels between the building of the ark and the building of the Tabernacle in the wilderness. Again, parallels are seen here with Noah's entering the ark and provisions made for the Tabernacle. Both were accompanied by animal sacrifices. Unblemished animals had to be offered to the LORD in the Tabernacle (Lev. 1:3, 10). Similarly, seven pairs of clean animals were taken into the ark, some of which were offered in sacrifice after the

Flood (Gen. 8:20). The need for clean, unblemished animals for sacrifices points us to the sinlessness of Christ who died for our sins,
that through our faith in him we might enter the presence of our
holy God.

Repeatedly, the Flood account told us that pairs of every kind of
animal entered the ark (6:19, 20; 7:2, 8, 9, 15, 16). Some see a con-
tradiction between the instruction for two of every kind of animal to
go into the ark in chapter 6 and seven pairs of clean animals commanded to enter in chapter 7. But this is easily resolved if we understand that the general instruction in chapter 6 was designed to
preserve God's animal creation from becoming extinct. The specific
instruction in chapter 7 was designed to provide animals for sacrifices
after the Flood (Gen. 8:20) and for food (Gen. 9:3). This distinction
between what was clean and unclean, holy and unholy was a feature
of the theocratic Israelite covenant community. It symbolically distinguished between the sanctified nation separated to God in
his kingdom and the nations outside that theocratic realm. Similarly,
this separation in the ark theocracy between God's covenant community and the world was symbolized by the clean/unclean distinction. It points to the all-pervasive attribute of God as holy. God
is set apart from us as the object of our awe, adoration, and dread.
As the people of his kingdom, we too are to be holy.

Yet the ark, which represented the visible kingdom of God, contained both clean and unclean animals. They represented, as ancient
church father Bede comments, "those in the church both spiritual and
carnal."[1] So the visible church contains both saved and unsaved until
the final judgment when the angels will throw in the fiery furnace all
who do evil (Matt. 13:24–30, 36–43). Only Jesus can ultimately dis-
cern the heart and faith of each person. As the ark was filled with
unclean animals along with the clean, just as profane Ham entered the
ark with the godly, so too the church has impure hypocrites creep-
ing into its outward communion.

Of the five categories of animals mentioned at creation (Gen. 1:21–25), four of them entered the ark: wild animals, livestock, creatures that move along the ground, and everything with wings. The creatures of the sea did not go in the ark, because they could survive in the water. The extent of the Flood was indicated by the fact that birds too were taken into the ark to be preserved. If the Flood were simply a localized event, they would be able to fly to dry land.

As God has given animals the instinct to migrate during changing seasons and to hibernate in winter, so he gave the animals the ability to come to the ark in pairs to be safe from the approaching flood. It may be that they sensed the changes happening in the atmosphere and tremors on the earth. For example, scientists have found that prior to an earthquake, cockroaches increase their activity. Whatever means God used, it was still a demonstration of his sovereign power that he was able to bring pairs of each kind of unclean animal and seven pairs of each clean animal into the ark.

God's care for his creation is evident in his preserving the animals in the ark. The wide diversity in the animals of the world illustrates the design, beauty, and creativity of our wonderful LORD. The fact that he purposely saved them indicates that we too ought to preserve animals from extinction by maintaining wildlife preserves and forests for our posterity to enjoy the same diversity of life. God is concerned for and cares for all his creation. As the pinnacle of God's creation, we have the responsibility of ruling over and caring for the rest of the creation (Gen. 1:26, 28).

It is interesting to see that the LORD chose to preserve pairs of all the animals in the ark. Could he not have just re-created the animals as he did at creation? Is there significance in their being included in the ark, too? If we agree that the ark was representative of the cosmic house of God, the eternal kingdom as a type, then including animals in the ark indicates that animals will also be in the

new heavens and new earth. This is confirmed in Isaiah's vision of
the peaceable kingdom:

> The wolf will live with the lamb,
>   the leopard will lie down with the goat,
> the calf and the lion and the yearling together;
>   and a little child will lead them.
> The cow will feed with the bear,
>   their young will lie down together,
>   and the lion will eat straw like the ox. (Isa. 11:6, 7)

Augustine of Hippo sees a typified role for the animals entering
the ark. "For why were all living creatures shut up in that ark except
to signify all the nations? For God did not lack the capability of creating anew every species of living things."[2] In God's intelligent
design, he loves variety in his creation, even among people. They
come in many varieties of color, height, size, and shape. Since all
the peoples of the world came from the household of Noah, all the
nations were truly in the ark. In this we see a type of our salvation
through the blood of the Lamb who died for the sins of the world
(John 1:29). Christ "purchased men for God from every tribe and
language and people and nation" (Rev. 5:9).

ᐭ Rain Fell Forty Days and Forty Nights

First, God warned that it would rain for forty days and forty nights
(Gen. 7:4). Then the account tells us this happened: "On that day
all the springs of the great deep burst forth, and the floodgates
of the heavens were opened. And rain fell on the earth forty days
and forty nights" (Gen. 7:11, 12). This time period of forty days and
nights often characterized a critical point in the history of redemption. At the time that Moses received the tablets with the Ten
Commandments, he fasted without eating or drinking for forty days

and nights on three occasions. He did so the first time he went up Mount Horeb to receive the commandments of the covenant (Deut. 9:9). Then on coming down the mountain and seeing the sinful behavior and idol worship of the Israelites, he fasted forty days and nights again (Deut. 9:18, 25). Finally, on going up Mount Horeb to receive the Ten Commandments a second time, Moses fasted again for forty days and nights (Deut. 10:10).

To the Israelites who did not believe that God could give them victory over those peoples who lived in the land of Canaan, the Lord had them wander in the wilderness for forty years and die so the next generation would be brought into the Promised Land. There may be an intentional parallel between the salvation of Noah and his family in the ark for forty days and nights of rain and the salvation represented by the Tabernacle among the Israelites for forty years in the wilderness. Both indicated the centrality of God's covenant relationship with his chosen people.[3]

After Jesus' baptism at the beginning of his public ministry, he was led into the wilderness where he fasted for forty days and nights. At the end of that period, Satan tempted Jesus to submit to his authority (Matt. 4:1–10). This was a crucial test as to whether Jesus would follow through with suffering and dying for the sins of the world so the will of the Father would be completed. But Jesus overcame temptation with the Word of God.

Finally, after Jesus' resurrection, he appeared to his disciples over a period of forty days before he ascended to heaven (Acts 1:3). He presented many convincing proofs that he was alive and thus prepared the church for the coming of the Holy Spirit. So the disciples who had been unconvinced came to the full conviction that Jesus had risen from the dead and that he truly was the Son of God. Thus, forty days and forty nights throughout biblical history were a significant time of testing and transition in the work of God among people.

Perhaps we have experienced a time of trial and testing. If not, it will surely come. Will we persevere? With the Lord's help, we will

(Isa. 43:2, 5). We cannot do it in our own strength. But soon the night will be over, and everything will be made clear in the light. Until that time, we continue to trust in the Lord. In coming through a time of testing, we know we will be further refined as gold or silver as the dross is cleaned out of our lives (Job 23:10; Isa. 48:10).

∿ Parallel Flood Accounts

"In the six hundredth year of Noah's life, on the seventeenth day of the second month—on that day all the springs of the great deep burst forth, and the floodgates of the heavens were opened" (Gen. 7:11). Note how this account was given with great detail as to when it occurred as by someone with a vivid memory of the events. Obviously, Moses must have received a recorded tablet of the events of the Flood, as he did concerning the other generations described both earlier and later, and he compiled them into the account we have in Genesis.

Interestingly, hundreds of other accounts of a great flood are found in diverse cultures around the world. Accounts are found in tribes in Papua New Guinea; among North American, South American, and Caribbean Indian tribes; among the natives of Africa, Greenland, and Hawaii; among the people of Wales, Lithuania, ancient Greece, ancient Egypt, India, and China. These traditions were not developed from Christian missionaries, as some have tried to explain this phenomenon. But flood accounts have been found among people groups that have never had any contact with Christianity or the Bible.

Studies made of ancient Chinese pictographs and ideographs from as long ago as 2500 BC appear to illustrate ancient oral traditions that parallel the Genesis account. Among the Chinese characters that illustrate Genesis, one has the figure of eight people on a boat. This character for eight has an important role in many Chinese characters that relate to the events surrounding the Flood. The various parts of one character mean *covered over* joined to *all* or *united* with *hands joined together* in rebellion to escape the threatening waters. When the radical for *water* is combined with that for *covered over*, it forms the word *to drown, to overflow, to be submerged*. The character for eight is added to *hands joined*, forming the word *total, altogether*. When one adds the radical for *water* to this character, it means *flood* or *vast*. This pictured a flood involving eight persons that was *total* or universal. After the flood, the eight were depicted in a character as living in a *cave*. Another character referred to the eight as *common to all, public*, defining the members of Noah's family. It also meant *grandfather*, indicating Noah as the grandfather of all living.[43]

James Boice describes a flood story from India that has much significant detail.

> In India the Hindus regard Manu as the progenitor of the race. He had been warned of the pending flood by a fish, who told him to build a ship and put into it all kinds of seeds, together with seven Rishis or holy beings. The Flood came. People drowned. But Manu's ship was drawn to safety by the fish who finally caused it to ground on the highest summits of the Himalayan Mountains. In this story eight people were saved, and Manu is called "righteous among his generation." Even more remarkable, the Hindus preserve a story in which Manu later became drunk and lay uncovered until cared for by two of his sons, a close retelling of the story found in Genesis 9:20–27.[5]

But the account that has caught the attention of historians the most is the long ancient Babylonian *Epic of Gilgamesh*, particularly Tablet 11, last of the series. The British Museum contains an Assyrian version on a clay tablet from the seventh century BC. It was discovered in Nineveh in a dig in 1853 but not translated until 1872. It had been part of the library of the Assyrian king Ashurbanipal when the Babylonians, Medes, and Scythians destroyed Nineveh in 612 BC. It was taken from an even older account called the *Atrakhasis Epic* from the third millennium BC. This account provides more details concerning the creation of men and women, their history up to the Flood, and the new society afterward. The fascinating thing about the *Epic of Gilgamesh* is the great number of similarities to the story found in Genesis. At least seventeen features may be found in common between the two accounts in generally the same order. Some believe there may be borrowing or direct influence between the two accounts. However, there is no solid evidence of such borrowing, and in all likelihood they simply reflected a common origin from the actual fact of the Flood.

In the *Atrakhasis Epic,* we have the reason for the flood in that the petty gods decided to destroy all humankind with a catastrophic flood because of their annoying noise, not allowing the chief god to sleep. But Atrakhasis was instructed in a dream to build a boat and to bring on board his family and the animals. When they were all aboard, the flood came and wiped out all humankind. Then Atrakhasis learned whether the land was inhabitable again by sending out birds: a raven, a dove, and a swallow. He offered a sacrifice to the gods after landing on a mountain. This pleased the gods who swore not to cause such destruction again. Other elements differ from the biblical account. But there was enough similarity to see that they both had a Mesopotamian background. A Sumerian text also gave a briefer version of the same Babylonian account. These accounts are important in establishing an independent testimony of there having been an ancient flood of catastrophic proportions. A variety of Babylonian writings referred to the Flood as being a particular point in time rather than being mere myth.

Since Abraham traveled from Ur to Canaan, he must have carried the Flood tradition along with the genealogy of his ancestors. All the numerous flood accounts around the world point to a common source of the events, no doubt in the memory of the descendants of Noah as they spread out from Mesopotamia. This gives witness to historical events that occurred in a devastating Deluge. As Barnabas and Paul said to the crowd in Lystra concerning God's witness to the nations, "Yet he has not left himself without testimony" (Acts 14:17).

The major difference between the biblical account and these others is in their moral and theological content. What God revealed through Moses were not just the facts but also their interpretation.[6] "With mixed standards of conduct on the part of the deities and a hazy view of sin, the Babylonian account quite naturally confuses the moral causes of the Flood, compromises the justice of it, and presents it more as the result of the caprice of the gods than as a necessary punishment of outrageous sin."[7] The *Gilgamesh Epic* focused on human heroes or mighty men and the gods, while the biblical account focused on the monotheism of the Lord and Noah's obedience. There also is a difference in moral attitude. We learn of Noah's faith and righteousness as the recipient of God's grace, and of our holy God's judgment of unrepentant sinners. The biblical account warned the wicked of their error and gave hope and comfort to those who fear God. The other accounts differ from the biblical one in the form and size of the ark, the duration of the Flood, and the order of sending out the birds. The implications of the commonalities between the Babylonian story and the biblical account indicate a common origin of a major catastrophic event early in history. But the interpretation of the events sets the biblical record apart as self-confirming special revelation from God rather than human myth or story.

∾ Literary Structure Reveals Redemption

"The animals going in were male and female of every living thing, as God had commanded Noah. Then the LORD shut him in" (Gen. 7:16). Higher critical scholars of the Bible portray Genesis as not written by Moses, but edited hundreds of years later after the Babylonian exile by priests who wove several different traditions into one document. This theory is called the documentary hypothesis, which goes by the initials J.E.D.P. for the Jehovist, Elohist,

Deuteronomic, and Priestly sections of the Pentateuch, the five books of the Torah.[8] Verse 16 is one of those verses they particularly note in which there is a change in the word used for God. The general name for God as Creator is *Elohim*. But the specific personal and covenant name of God as Redeemer is *Yahweh* or *Jehovah*, translated as LORD in the New International Version. The higher critical scholars say that having both names of God in verse 16 is an indication of two different documents being integrated together, namely the P and J accounts.

However, it is clear that God the Creator, *Elohim*, commanded Noah to bring pairs of creatures into the ark to preserve his creation. But the LORD as Redeemer, *Yahweh*, who closed the door of the ark, kept them safe from judgment. The different word usage for God was deliberate by the author to further illustrate the LORD's redemptive role.

More recent scholars have shown that the repetitions of numerous phrases in the Flood account are not just found twice, indicating two sources, but are often repeated three, four, and even five times. Thus, it is illogical to analyze the story on the basis of two documents. Rather the constant repetition provides a dramatic effect on the narrative. This is called "epic repetition."

In fact, the whole literary structure of the Deluge account is made up of seven parts from 6:13 to 8:22. Each part is distinguished by a different theme arranged in a delta-type pattern of correspondences. The first (6:13–22) and seventh (8:20–22), second (7:1–5) and sixth (8:15–19), and third (7:6–12) and fifth (8:1–14) sections correspond with themes of construction—consecration, embarkation—disembarkation and the increasing waters—decreasing waters and drying out. They culminate in the climactic fourth section (7:13–24) concerning the prevailing judgment waters over the earth. Each section is marked by opening-closing patterns. Additionally, sections two through six reveal remarkable literary artistry in the progressively rising structure from two to four with a reverse form in five to six. So rather than being clumsy repetitions from poor redaction of supposed multiple-source material, we have a masterpiece of literary form using a chiastic structure. Meredith Kline describes this feature saying, "There is thus a literary heightening from a one- to a two- and then a three-level structure, and this rising and peaking literary form structurally mirrors the physical scene it is describing, with the continual increasing of the waters to their mountain covering crest."[9]

⌇ The LORD Shut Them in

After Noah, his family, and all the animals had gone into the ark, "Then the LORD shut him in" (Gen. 7:16). The significance of this is that it revealed God as the chief actor in these events. As opposed to the Babylonian Flood account where the hero shut the door of the ark, God separated his own from the rest of the world and protected them. In shutting the door, God made a distinction between the righteous and the wicked, the saved and the lost. We see God's sovereign work of definite redemption taking place in his plan to save only Noah and his family from judgment.

In the LORD shutting the door, we see another aspect of Noah's walk with God. On numerous occasions, God revealed himself to Noah. He was with Noah and spoke to him. He was there to protect Noah from the chaos of the waters and the ensuing destruction. As Yahweh, the covenant-keeping Redeemer God, he sealed the door to ensure Noah's household's salvation. This action is a type of the work of "the Holy Spirit of God, with whom [we] were sealed for the day of redemption" (Eph. 4:30). That seal guarantees our spiritual inheritance (2 Cor. 5:5).

The opportunity to enter the ark was given for all who would repent of their sins and believe the Lord's message through Noah. God's grace is great. There is a free offer of the gospel to all who will believe. Although Noah preached for 120 years, no one believed his message of coming judgment. Instead, they persecuted the righteous.

They refused to repent and come to the ark because their deeds were evil. Those who do evil love the darkness. "Everyone who does evil hates the light, and will not come into the light for fear that his deeds will be exposed" (John 3:20).

The image of a protecting door separating the righteous from the wicked is found numerous times in the Scriptures. Angels pulled Lot into his house and shut the door to protect him from the evil men outside (Gen. 19:10). The angel of death did not kill the Israelites' firstborn sons when he saw the blood of the lamb on their doorframes, while he killed the Egyptians' firstborn (Exod. 12:23). Rahab and her family were protected behind the door of their house while the Israelites destroyed the rest of Jericho (Josh. 2:19). Jesus, too, used the image of a shut door regarding the five foolish virgins who went to buy oil for their lamps just before the bridegroom arrived. The five wise virgins went into the wedding banquet, and the door was shut behind them. Then the foolish virgins pleaded to be let in, but the bridegroom replied, "I don't know you" (Matt. 25:10–12). The time of entering God's kingdom had passed.

Isaiah gave us a direct reference to God shutting in Noah for protection. The remnant of Judah were to take refuge from the coming judgment through the Assyrian oppressors and the Babylonian exile.

> Go, my people, enter your rooms
>   and shut the doors behind you;
> hide yourselves for a little while
>   until his wrath has passed by. (Isa. 26:20)

As with Noah, the righteous remnant were to wait in safety from the LORD's indignation. Similarly, if we are under persecution and suffering for our faith, we know that the Lord is our refuge and strength. Jesus will protect us from his wrath that will come on the wicked (1 Thess. 1:10; 2 Pet. 2:9).

The imagery goes further if we understand the shutting of doors behind us as a time in death until the resurrection (Isa. 26:19). This corresponds with the typology of Noah and his family being saved through water as a baptism (1 Pet. 3:20, 21) for in baptism we identify ourselves with Jesus' death (Rom. 6:3, 4). Noah being shut in the ark was a type of his passing through death to sin. It was one element of the covenant God made with Noah before he entered the ark (Gen. 6:18).

As the sky looked ominous, the thunder rumbled, and the lightning flashed, the crowd of sinners that once ridiculed Noah began to worry. Then the rain came down in torrents. As the waters rose and streamed into their homes, people must have fled for refuge to the ark. Screaming and pounding on the door, they pled for entrance, but they could not get in.

This is a warning for people today, for judgment is coming. Once the door is shut, no one will open it. There will be no second chance. Although the Lord's grace is great, there is an end to grace. There was one final week when the people saw the animals and Noah's family go into the ark. On the seventh day, most likely the Sabbath, they entered God's rest in the ark. Jonathan Edwards used this event as a warning to each of us.

> You have been once more warned today, while the door of the ark yet stands open. You have, as it were, once again heard the knocks of the hammer and axe in the building of the ark, to put you in mind that a flood is approaching. Take heed therefore that you do not still stop your ears, treat these warnings with a regardless heart, and still neglect the great work which you have to do, lest the flood of wrath suddenly come upon you, sweep you away, and there be no remedy.[10]

The author of Hebrews likewise warned us, "Since the promise of entering his rest still stands, let us be careful that none of you be found to have fallen short of it" (Heb. 4:1). "Those who formerly had the gospel preached to them did not go in, because of their disobedience. . . . Let us, therefore, make every effort to enter that rest, so that no one will fall by following their example of disobedience" (Heb. 4:6, 11). The people had a chance to repent under Noah's preaching and seek refuge in the ark. But then the day of reckoning came. The week ended, the door was shut, and the rain began to pour.

Until now God has been patient with us, "not wanting anyone to perish," but that all his elect[11] come to repentance (2 Pet. 3:9). Today is the day of salvation (2 Cor. 6:2). Now is our opportunity to find refuge in Christ. He provides a secure refuge against the wrath of God that will be revealed from heaven (Rom. 1:18; 5:9). Come to him, and he will not drive us away (John 6:37). As the LORD said to Noah, "Come into the ark . . ." (Gen. 7:1 NKJV), Jesus says to us, "Come to me, all you who are weary and burdened, and I will give you rest" (Matt. 11:28).

SCRIPTURE READING:
ISAIAH 26

Discussion Questions

1. How was Noah and his family entering the ark a prototype of our salvation?
2. What is the significance of the distinction between clean and unclean animals?
3. What significance is found in the rain falling for forty days and nights? How may the testing of our faith purify it?
4. How have numerous flood accounts around the world confirmed an ancient flood tradition?
5. How has the author of the Deluge account used a literary style of repetition to enhance the movement and impact of the story? How does understanding this refute the documentary hypothesis?

6. What significance do we find in the LORD shutting the door of the ark? What comfort do you receive from this?

7. As Noah entered God's rest in the ark, how may we do so as well?

Notes

1. Andrew Louth, ed., *Genesis 1–11*, OT vol. 1 of *Ancient Christian Commentary on Scripture* (Downers Grove, Ill.: InterVarsity, 2001), 142.

2. Ibid., 136.

3. John Sailhamer, "Genesis," in vol. 2 of *The Expositor's Bible Commentary*, ed. Frank E. Gaebelein (Grand Rapids: Zondervan, 1990), 85.

4. C. H. Kang and Ethel R. Nelson, *The Discovery of Genesis* (St. Louis: Concordia, 1979), 95–100.

5. James Montgomery Boice, *Genesis*, vol. 1 of *An Expositional Commentary* (Grand Rapids: Zondervan, 1982), 284.

6. Alan Millard, "Flood Stories," in *Eerdmans' Handbook to the Bible*, eds. David Alexander and Patricia Alexander (Grand Rapids: Eerdmans, 1973), 133.

7. Merrill F. Unger, *Archaeology and the Old Testament* (Grand Rapids: Zondervan, 1954), 67.

8. There is no external evidence for the critical source hypothesis, but it has been derived solely from internal evidence. Therefore, it is speculation for those who hold to this hypothesis to believe the biblical text is simply a product of religious consciousness in Israel rather than divine revelation. Additionally, Jesus affirmed that Moses wrote the Pentateuch (Mark 12:26; Luke 24:27, 44).

9. Meredith G. Kline, *Kingdom Prologue* (Overland Park, Kans.: Two Age Press, 2000), 214.

10. Mark Water, comp., *The New Encyclopedia of Christian Quotations* (Grand Rapids: Baker, 2000), 539.

11. Looking at this verse in its context, we see that it is not speaking of the salvation of all people, but only about Christians, called "dear friends" (2 Pet. 3:1, 8) who are to make their "calling and election sure" (1:10). Note that the LORD is patient with "you," who had been confused by false teachers. They misunderstood that all things do not continue without intervention from God (as in the Flood) and that God is long-suffering. In light of the LORD's coming, God is patiently waiting for all the elect to come to repentance, many of whom are still in future generations. Jesus will lose none of those given to him by the Father (John 6:39).

The Extent
of the Flood

Genesis 7:17–23

17 *For forty days the flood kept coming on the earth, and as the waters increased they lifted the ark high above the earth.* **18** *The waters rose and increased greatly on the earth, and the ark floated on the surface of the water.* **19** *They rose greatly on the earth, and all the high mountains under the entire heavens were covered.* **20** *The waters rose and covered the mountains to a depth of more than twenty feet.* **21** *Every living thing that moved on the earth perished—birds, livestock, wild animals, all the creatures that swarm over the earth, and all mankind.* **22** *Everything on dry land that had the breath of life in its nostrils died.* **23** *Every living thing on the face of the earth was wiped out; men and animals and the creatures that move along the ground and the birds of the air were wiped from the earth. Only Noah was left, and those with him in the ark.*

FROM THE BEGINNING of the account of Noah, God shared his intention with him to destroy the earth (Gen. 6:7). He repeated his intention three more times (Gen. 6:13, 17; 7:4). Then we are told, "Every living thing on the face of the earth was wiped out" (Gen. 7:23). But could this destruction have meant simply a local flood in Mesopotamia, or was the flood of global proportions? This has been a difficult question to answer from our present knowledge of prehistory apart from the Scriptures.

What we do know is that God preserved the lives of Noah, his family, and pairs of animals in the ark from a catastrophic Deluge. Through the Flood, God gloriously triumphed over his enemies. It was a flood of judgment against the wickedness of humanity and Satan's dominion over them. Judgment is sure to come again by fire, although we may be oblivious to the signs of its coming.

～ God Determined to Destroy the Earth

God first spoke to Noah about his intention to destroy the earth by flood at the beginning of the 120 years left for people to live (Gen. 6:3, 5–7). This would have been before Noah's three sons were born. Noah was five hundred years old when he became the father of Shem, Ham, and Japheth (5:32). This does not mean his sons were all born the same year but after he was five hundred years old. He was six hundred years old when the Flood came (7:6, 11). Consequently, it appears that verses of chapter 6 were a series of God's instructions to Noah over the course of those 120 years, for Noah's sons and their wives were included in God's covenant (6:18).

God determined to destroy life on the whole earth (6:7, 13, 17). All the animals had to suffer God's judgment as well. Repeatedly, universal language was used to describe the extent of the Flood's destruction. "The LORD said, 'I will wipe mankind, whom I have created, from the face of the earth' " (6:7). "So God said to Noah, 'I am going to put an end to all people' " (6:13).

" 'I am going to bring floodwaters on the earth to destroy all life under the heavens, every creature that has the breath of life in it. Everything on earth will perish' " (6:17). In the following three chapters, we continue to see universal language used (7:4, 21ff.; 8:21; 9:11, 15).

∽ Local Flood Viewpoint

Many Bible scholars believe the Flood was extensive but merely regional rather than global. In support of this viewpoint, several places in Scripture use universal terminology with a more limited sense, such as the famine during the time of Joseph (Gen. 41:56ff.); the extent of King Nebuchadnezzar's rule (Dan. 2:38; 4:22; 5:19); "Jews from every nation under heaven" (Acts 2:5); "All over the world this gospel is bearing fruit" (Col. 1:6); "The gospel . . . that has been proclaimed to every creature under heaven" (Col. 1:23). At times hyperbole was used to dramatize the extent of what was described and to make the point that the spread of the gospel was not just local or regional but worldwide. The events of the Flood would also be from the limited perspective of the eight who were on the ark, for which it would appear the whole earth was covered or "from the standpoint of Moses' geographic knowledge."[1]

Archeologist Leonard Woolley claimed that a flood about four thousand years ago covered an area northwest of the Persian Gulf four hundred miles long and one hundred miles wide. (However, subsequent archeologists have questioned the extent of this flood.) This would have been the inhabitants' whole world. The word *earth* may have a more restrictive meaning of "land" in a regional sense. "All life under the heavens" (Gen. 6:17) could be understood as all life within the range of Noah's perception. So those advocating a local or regional flood say that universal expressions used in ancient times could not be taken in the same sense as our modern language. Noah's preaching of righteousness was not to the peoples of Africa,

India, China, or the Americas, for there is much evidence of human life in those parts prior to the estimated time of the Flood.

The perspective of the author of Genesis was to write about the culture and peoples from which Abraham eventually came. He was narrating from his own perspective with the usual frame of reference of his ancient readers. His writing was factual in that it was based on an ancient Flood tradition, but it was symbolic in that it used that tradition as a vehicle to teach important redemptive truths, that sin leads to destruction and salvation comes from God alone.

As far as physical evidence for the Flood being regional, certain discoveries have been proposed to confirm this. In 1954 Sir Leonard Woolley published *Excavations at Ur* in which he claimed to have found incontrovertible evidence of the Genesis Flood. In his excavations at the ancient city of Ur in lower Mesopotamia in 1929, he found an eight-foot stratum of clean clay between levels of archeological finds. This indicated a great flood. A couple of hundred miles to the north, a similar discovery was made at Kish. However, later it was found through pottery above and below the flood strata that these two evidences of a great flood did not occur in the same century. Nor did the flood in Ur cover the entire city.[2]

In September 2000, a well-preserved structure that may be thousands of years old was discovered in the Black Sea twelve miles off the coast of Turkey, near Sinop, three hundred feet below sea level. Well-preserved carved wooden beams, wooden branches, and stone tools were in a collapsed wood-and-clay structure. A second site contained pieces of ceramics, giving evidence of Neolithic life on the day of the Flood. Scientists believe that through rapid melting of glaciers in Europe seven thousand years ago, the Mediterranean Sea rose, gushed through the narrow Bosphorus, and caused a much smaller freshwater lake to become the Black Sea. The dating of this flood and finding the ancient shoreline has been through shells of an extinct type of freshwater creature, all of which are seven thousand years old or older, while shells of saltwater shellfish date from

6,500 years ago.[3] This date fits well with the timing of the Flood, according to many who have made such estimations.

However, dating the Flood is difficult, especially if one takes the view that the genealogical tables of Genesis 10 and 11 contain large gaps between generations, with only the most prominent figures being named.[4] The nations descending from Noah's sons imply an early date for the Flood of some millennia before the Babylonian floods of around 3,000 BC.[5] Some have pointed out that the Flood must have been prior to the proven beginnings of civilizations in Egypt and Mesopotamia around 4,000 BC that show no evidence of a major break since then. In fact, Jericho and Jarmo have undisturbed remains dating back to the eighth millennium BC. Francis Schaeffer suggests that the Flood must be dated prior to 20,000 BC for two reasons. First, the lack of chronology in the Genesis genealogies makes this possible. Second, most anthropologists estimate Indians entered North America around 20,000 BC across the Bering Strait. Since they would be descendants of Noah, the Flood must have taken place prior to this time. Both North and South American Indians have flood myth traditions.[6]

Davis A. Young advocates a contrary view, writing,

> Archeology has firmly demonstrated that the civilization described in Genesis 4 was in place by at least 6000 B.C., thus constraining the biblical deluge to a date more recent than that, and evidence associated with the Gilgamesh epic seems to imply that the biblical deluge would have to have occurred closer to 3000 B.C. Archeological evidence rules out the occurrence of a widespread deluge ten or twenty thousand years ago. Most of those who support the notion that a deluge occurred at that more distant date are seeking to establish the viability of an event that, even if confined to the Near East, could have destroyed the whole human race. But archeological investigations have established the presence of human beings in the Americas, Australia, and southeastern Asia

long before the advent of the sort of Near Eastern civilization described in the Bible and thus long before the biblical deluge could have taken place. In the light of a wealth of mutually supportive evidence from a variety of disciplines and sources, it is simply no longer tenable to insist that a deluge drowned every human on the face of the globe except Noah's family.[7]

However, a weakness I find with this argument is that if one starts with the premise of a worldwide Flood, archeological evidence for the description of the development of agriculture and metallurgy in Genesis 4:20–22 would have been destroyed but reappeared after the Flood. Therefore, it provides no proof for a more recent date for the Flood. Actually, even a recent date that was regional in scope would have been noted in the tells of ancient civilizations. Such evidence of a flood over an extensive region has yet to be found.

One may ask, could not the Flood have been simply regional in scope, yet still have killed all humanity, except for the eight in the ark, by the likelihood that humanity had not yet spread over all the earth?[8] Noah was a "preacher of righteousness" to all of them. This regional possibility seems to be confirmed by the later account of the people at Babel attempting to build a tower up to the heavens. All the people spoke one language, an indication of people groups not living isolated from other groups, as happens in the development of various dialects and languages. Then the LORD scattered them over all the earth by confusing their language (Gen. 11:8, 9). God's purpose was that humanity should "fill the earth and subdue it" (Gen. 1:28). Possibly prior to the Flood, this mandate was not being fully fulfilled.

Other problems of physical limitations and logistics make the universal Flood viewpoint difficult for many to accept. Where could the tremendous volume of water needed to cover all the high mountains have come from and then disappeared to after the Flood? The polar ice caps and the atmosphere do not contain sufficient water to cover the earth to a depth of over three miles (Mount Ararat) or more if we include major peaks like Mount Everest. How could all the sea life and freshwater life live together in brackish water? How could fish that can only survive at tremendous depths have survived the Flood if the earth's surface was much flatter prior to the Flood, as some global Flood advocates believe? How could animals that survive uniquely in one particular climate (rainforest or polar regions) or on a specialized diet (such as koala bears who eat only fresh eucalyptus leaves) survive for a year on the ark? How did those animals travel thousands of miles to the ark and then travel thousands of miles back to islands, deserts, jungles, and mountains to which they were adapted to live? Could the 4,500 species of living mammals and 8,650 species of living birds with all their year's food supply have fit on the ark and survived? Besides the land animals and birds, did Noah also take on the ark a pair of about one million species of insects we know of today? Some of these questions may remain unanswerable this side of heaven so all are convinced. As Solomon wrote, "[God] has also set eternity in the hearts of men; yet they cannot fathom what God has done from beginning to end" (Eccles. 3:11).

∼ Universal Flood Viewpoint

Despite the above arguments, many who take God's Word seriously believe the Scriptures teach a worldwide Flood. God's explicit language is quoted as being universal. In Genesis 6–9, the universality of the Flood and its effects are expressed over thirty times. The Flood's universality is not incidental but of primary importance to the author. It is seen in the tenor of the whole narrative. God gave his perspective in the account, not people's limited perspective, as in the earlier anthropomorphisms describing God (Gen. 6:6). In the literary structure of Genesis, the first eleven chapters deal with universal origins, while the remaining chapters (12–50) concentrate on the origin of the Hebrew nation. Three and a half of those first eleven chapters deal with the Flood, while creation is dealt with in only two chapters. In the era after the Flood, we are told that the nations developing from Noah's three sons spread out over the earth (9:19; 10:32). Nations mentioned arising from their descendants are in Asia, Africa, and Europe, indicating extensive depopulation from the Flood in those areas. So from this literary structure, we see the tremendous magnitude of a universal Flood.

If the Flood were only a localized catastrophe, why save pairs of animals in the ark, particularly the birds, which could fly to safety? The LORD told Noah to take into the ark "male and female, to keep their various kinds alive throughout the earth" (Gen. 7:3). This would only be necessary if the Flood were global. Would there have been room on the ark? With 1,500,000 cubic feet of space in the ark, it could easily hold representatives of every air-breathing mammal, bird, and reptile and their provisions. This would represent perhaps a total of 16,000 animals that would reproduce after their *kinds*. The wide variety of species has since been produced through microevolution, which continually occurs today.[9] I would assume this argument would mean a very ancient date for the Flood.

After the Flood, when God made his covenant promise to Noah not to ever destroy the earth again by a flood, God's common-grace covenant loses its meaning if he were speaking of the Flood in Noah's day as only being localized. We still have large floods today that destroy almost whole countries, and many thousands of people and animals have died. It would be ironic to see the rainbow after such a flood. Then what would be the meaning of God's promise to never destroy the earth by flood again? His covenant promise was universal, to never again cover the earth with water or to destroy all living creatures as he had done (Gen. 8:21; 9:11; Isa. 54:9).

Jesus, too, in speaking of the unexpected timing of his return, said, "The flood came and took them *all* away" (Matt. 24:39, emphasis added; cf. Luke 17:27). The force of Jesus' argument that we must *all* be ready would be gone if some people escaped the destruction of the Flood or if the fire and sulfur that rained down on Sodom did not destroy them *all*. When the apostle Peter spoke of the Flood, he assumed a worldwide flood, saying, "By these waters also the world of that time was deluged and destroyed" (2 Pet. 3:6). He then compared it to the present heavens and earth, which are reserved for fire. He is not saying that only one localized area would be burned in the final judgment. To make Peter's comparison sensible, he implied that just as the Flood was global, so the final judgment by fire will be global.

If only part of the human race were destroyed by the Flood, the major point made in Scripture of *all* humanity being corrupt, violent, and having hearts inclined toward evil would be lost. Noah and his family being saved because of God's covenant love would not be anything unique or special, for many others not affected by the Flood would not have suffered God's judgment. God preserved Noah and his family to continue his promises to Adam and Eve of a Redeemer for people and to make a fresh start with the human race through Noah and his descendants.

The physical effects of the Flood are difficult for local-flood advocates to overcome without an explanation of major changes in the crust of the earth. "All the high mountains under the entire heavens were covered. The waters rose and covered the mountains to a depth of more than twenty [-two and a half] feet" (Gen. 7:19, 20). If the ark came to rest on the Ararat Mountains (Gen. 8:4) at a height of seventeen thousand feet above sea level, it would be physically impossible for the waters not to cover the entire earth to a depth of up to three miles. If the solid earth were completely smooth, it would be covered to a depth of nine thousand feet of water everywhere. Catastrophic-flood theorists believe all mountains prior to the Flood did not exceed five thousand feet high. If one should argue that Moses wrote of an extensive flood from his limited regional knowledge of the world, even that does not seem reasonable. How could a flood be contained that extended from

Egypt to over the high mountains of Ararat, which covered everything, without spreading to the rest of the world?

We see in the description of the physical causes of the Flood a world-engulfing cataclysmic event. When the Flood began, "all the springs of the great deep burst forth" (Gen. 7:11). This may have involved great geological transformations with earthquakes, the shifting of the earth's crust, and perhaps the lowering of land and the rising of the seabed. Most mountains consist of sedimentary layers first laid down flat by water, which were later tipped and buckled. Since springs bursting forth were mentioned first, some have thought the displacement of vast underground water may have been the principle cause for the flooding. Solomon may be speaking of this event when he described the wisdom and knowledge of God saying, "By his knowledge the deeps broke open" (Prov. 3:20 ESV). Up to the time of the Flood, underground water had been the means for watering the earth along with a rising mist (Gen. 2:5, 6).

Walt Brown advocates a hydroplate theory, which assumes

> that (1) about 10 miles below interconnected continents was a large shell of salty, subterranean water, and (2) pressure was increasing within that water. . . .
>
> Water exploded with great violence out of the ten-mile-deep "slit" that wrapped around the earth like the seam of a baseball. . . .
>
> Much of the water fragmented into an "ocean" of droplets that fell as rain great distances away. This produced torrential rains such as the earth has never experienced—before or after. Some jetting water rose above the atmosphere where it froze and then fell on various regions of the earth as huge masses of extremely cold, muddy "hail." That hail buried, suffocated, and froze many animals, including some mammoths.[10]

However, there is some hesitation in this explanation in that geologists have not been able to find evidence for enough subterranean water reserves to flood the earth. Also, besides the Grand Canyon, not enough evidence exists for this "ten-mile-deep slit" out of which came the blast of water.

To produce a forty-day downpour of rain must have involved radical atmospheric and climatic changes. Those who hold to a young-earth theory see evidence for this in the fossils from warm-climate flora and fauna and the coal and oil found in Arctic regions. A protective vapor covering the earth kept a uniform and ideal climate but then partially provided the water for the rain in the Flood. After the forty-day downpour, rain continued for one hundred and fifty days as ordinary rain from evaporation and condensation (Gen. 7:24). Following the Flood, radical climatic changes caused sudden freezing of polar regions, proven by the discovery of numerous frozen mammoths and other animals.

Finally, why would Noah, his household, and the animals stay on the ark for over a year for a local flood? This is not logical. However, it makes good sense if the Flood were global. Much of the receding water must have become ice in the polar regions during the waiting period.

Uniformitarians, however, refute these claims by noting that mammoths were native to colder latitudes. They died from various natural causes such as falling over cliffs or into crevasses or getting caught in blizzards or mudflows that quickly preserved them. They died at various times, between 11,450 to 39,000 years ago, according to radiocarbon dating. This gives a strong indication that the north tundra region has remained frozen all this time, meaning it has not been covered by a flood since then.

The vapor-canopy theory assumes an abrupt change in climatic conditions from subtropical to the ice age. But "a variety of sources indicates that continental glaciers of the ice age built up, advanced, and retreated over long periods of time." Although subtropical conditions did exist in the northern areas at one time, the time of when they prevailed is an important factor.[11]

∽ Uniformitarian Geological Position

It is evident that resolving the extent of the Flood is a difficult question to answer from a scientific perspective. Both positions have major problems. A full discussion is beyond the scope of this book. However, to hold to a universal flood position does not seem to require one to hold to the Whitcomb-Morris theory of geological catastrophe advocated by many creationists. This theory contravenes much generally accepted geological evidence. Davis A. Young, a Christian geologist with a high view of Scripture, provides an alternative uniformitarian view.[12] Additionally, it should be noted that to hold to an uniformitarian view does not necessitate belief in the evolutionary theory and all that implies, even though evolutionists in other fields of science maintain uniformitarianism as well. For Christians who believe in an inerrant Scripture, holding to an uniformitarian view of geology fits best with a "framework hypothesis" understanding of the days of creation,[13] rather than holding to the "twenty-four-hour day" view.

Young gives four major critiques of the neocatastrophic flood geology.[14] First, there is a problem with explaining heat flow from crystallizing magmas of igneous rock that takes from hundreds of years to a million years to cool to surface temperatures, depending on size. The catastrophic flood theory requires that all thick layers of magma crystallize in less than the one-year Flood period, since samples of magma have intruded fossil dinosaur tracks and fossil fish. Additionally, there is overlain on the magma sill of the Palisades of New Jersey thick sequences of fossiliferous unconsolidated sand, clay, and gravel. Moreover, the magma sill was eroded prior to these deposits, indicating it cooled before being overlain by these formations. All of this process would not be possible within the year of the Flood with the same scientific laws in operation today.

Second, there are problems with the results of radioactive dating of igneous bodies that have intruded fossiliferous sedimentary formations. The Whitcomb-Morris theory has sought to discredit radioactive age dating by accusing those who do so of using pure guesswork because they do not know the amount of a radiogenic daughter element in a rock at the time of its formation. However, the rubidium-strontium isochron method, based on the radioactive decay of rubidium 87 (Rb^{87}) into strontium 87 (Sr^{87}), eliminates the guesswork of how much Sr^{87} was initially present in the rock as it was formed. The results of hundreds of tests have yielded ages of hundreds of millions of years for the crystallization of granite. This type of analysis has been found to agree with most relative ages of materials determined by only geological or paleontological criteria. The neocatastrophists have argued that at the time of the Flood, rocks have been given apparent age by a great increase in cosmic ray influx that led to greatly increased radioactive decay. However, studies of meteorites and moon rocks have shown that the effects of cosmic rays coming in from space only penetrate a few feet into a solid body. Therefore, the effect of cosmic rays on the radiometric age indicators of rocks that have formed thousands of feet or several miles below the surface of the earth would be insignificant.

Third, evidence from the study of the stability of metamorphic rocks found from the ranges of temperature and pressure they must have undergone makes the catastrophic view untenable. Metamorphic rock is formed from sedimentary and volcanic rock prior to being metamorphosed under extreme temperature and pressure. On rare occasions, fossils have even been found in these metamorphic rocks. According to the catastrophic flood theory, these fossils would have been deposited during the year of the Flood. Also, in southern New England, metamorphosed rock is overlain in places by unmetamorphosed fossiliferous sedimentary rocks. Dr. Young, in explaining the formation of metamorphosed rock in New England, says, "Hence the flood geologist is under the obligation of explaining in terms of his theory how it would have been possible *in less than one year* for the New England rocks to be heated to around 600°C and cooled back down to surface temperature, as well as buried to a depth of around twelve miles and brought all the way back to the surface!"[15]

Fourth, the theories of continental drift and seafloor spreading, known as global tectonics, provide a strong opposition to the Whitcomb-Morris flood theory. The plate tectonics theory holds that the continents of South America, Africa, India, Australia, and Antarctica were once all joined together as a single landmass. The northern landmass consisted of North America, Greenland, Europe, and Asia. The landmasses moved apart slowly, at the rate of a couple of centimeters per year, and continue to do so today. Evidence for the drift is seen in part by the remarkable fit of the coasts of the continents, particularly their continental shelves, as in a jigsaw puzzle. The trends of folds and faults, along with radiometric ages from South America to Africa give strong indications for continental drift.

Other evidences for continental drift are found in the continuity of mountain ranges when continents are rejoined; signs of a large continental glacial ice cap over a supercontinent; anorthosite rock bodies arranged in linear chains when seen in predrift reconstruction of the continents; seafloor mountain ranges formed along the point of rupture of the continents; and the oldest sediments on the Atlantic Ocean floor being from the relatively new Jurassic age. The building of the Rocky, Sierra Nevada, and Andes Mountains is due to the plowing and buckling of continents with oceanic crust. The Himalayan Mountain belt is due to the Indian landmass leaving the African continent and colliding with the Asian landmass. All this evidence for continental drift is impossible to be accommodated by the Whitcomb-Morris theory unless it was a pure miracle. The catastrophic flood theory would have to say that the continents were joined together before the Flood and even at the beginning of it. This is because glaciated Permian rock is fossil bearing.

But there is no evidence for an extremely rapid rate of continental drift. Rather, sediments with fossils were still being deposited and deformed during the formation of mountains from the collision of continents with oceanic crusts or other continents. This would mean that the formation of these uplifts had to take place in less than one year according to the Whitcomb-Morris theory. How could the continents then drift hundreds or thousands of miles within a period of a few months?

An interesting detail that affects the interpretation of the effects of the Flood is that God instructed Noah in constructing the ark to "coat it with pitch inside and out" (Gen. 6:14). Pitch is bitumen commonly found in Mesopotamia. It was used in the construction of the Tower of Babel (Gen. 11:3). Catastrophic Flood adherents theorize that such products as pitch and petroleum were produced as a result of the Flood rather than over a long period of geological history. Yet here Noah used it prior to the Flood.[16]

Scriptural evidence does not require that the Flood was a major geological event that ran counter to natural revelation. Extrabiblical evidence needs more study to further our understanding of this difficult topic. True biblical interpretation of the Flood will agree with true science. At times, good extrabiblical scientific evidence may affect our biblical interpretation.[17] God's purpose is not to give us a scientific explanation for these events. We accept them as true by faith. However, he has given us intellects to apply our knowledge of the world to understand spiritual truth through his general revelation. Solomon did just that, and people came from many nations to hear his wisdom regarding the natural world (1 Kings 4:33, 34). Although we will never fully understand all the questions raised by Scripture, the main point of the biblical account is that the Flood was God's *total* cataclysmic judgment on wicked humanity. However, it was a means of deliverance for Noah and his household, who were recipients of God's grace. In knowing that we, too, have received God's grace, we can rejoice, trusting God for our unanswered questions.

⌇ The LORD's Glorious Triumph

For forty days, rain continued to come down on the earth, and water
rose up from the ground. "The waters rose and increased greatly on
the earth" (Gen. 7:18). The word *rose* is translated in the NKJV and
ESV as "prevailed." The Hebrew word used has a military significance for triumph in battle. God's judgment prevailed over the
objects of his wrath because of their sin. He triumphed gloriously
over his enemies. David praised the LORD with allusions to his triumph in the Flood:

> The voice of the LORD is over the waters;
>> the God of glory thunders,
>> the LORD thunders over the mighty waters. . . .
> The voice of the LORD strikes
>> with flashes of lightning. . . .
> The LORD sits enthroned over the flood;
>> the LORD is enthroned as King forever. (Ps. 29:3, 7, 10)

The Lord's dominion is what we can expect in the day of judgment
to come. No person or demonic power will be able to withstand his
terrible destruction and victorious power over his creation. This is
what we will see when Jesus is on the great white throne at the end
of the age:

> The sea gave up the dead that were in it, and death and Hades
> gave up the dead that were in them, and each person was judged
> according to what he had done. Then death and Hades were
> thrown into the lake of fire. The lake of fire is the second death.
> If anyone's name was not found written in the book of life, he was
> thrown into the lake of fire." (Rev. 20:13–15)

This is the triumph of God in his judgment. All God's enemies will
be thrown into the lake of fire.

David made allusion to the power of God at the Flood and the Exodus when he sang praise to God for his victory over his enemies.

> The earth trembled and quaked,
>> and the foundations of the mountains shook;
>> they trembled because he was angry. . . .
> He parted the heavens and came down;
>> dark clouds were under his feet.
> He mounted the cherubim and flew;
>> he soared on the wings of the wind.
> He made darkness his covering, his canopy around him—
>> the dark rain clouds of the sky.
> Out of the brightness of his presence clouds advanced,
>> with hailstones and bolts of lightning.
> The LORD thundered from heaven;
>> the voice of the Most High resounded.
> He shot his arrows and scattered the enemies,
>> great bolts of lightning and routed them.
> The valleys of the sea were exposed
>> and the foundations of the earth laid bare
> at your rebuke, O LORD,
>> at the blast of breath from your nostrils. (Ps. 18:7, 9–15)

This fearful theophany of the Divine Warrior depicts him as sweeping down on his enemies as a fierce thunderstorm. No one can withstand the wrath of God against his foes. However, Noah (as we who believe) was reconciled with God through faith in the death of the promised Messiah, although this was still only seen by type. So rather than being God's enemy, Noah was now his son and friend.

"The waters rose and increased greatly on the earth, and the ark floated on the surface of the water" (Gen. 7:18). Here we see a contrast between the waters of judgment and the waters that bore the ark to safety. Donald Barnhouse comments on how this illustrates that "the same judgment that swept down from God upon the Lord Jesus Christ brings death to those who refuse and life to those who believe. In the ark Noah was surrounded by judgment, which showed God's hatred of sin, but he himself was safe. In Christ we are surrounded by the judgment of God against sin, and we are safe."[18]

∼ Every Living Thing Perished

The judgment during the Flood is a prototype of the judgment yet to come on all who refuse to repent of their sins, to submit to the lordship of Christ, and to walk with God by faith.

> Every living thing that moved on the earth perished—birds, livestock, wild animals, all the creatures that swarm over the earth, and all mankind. Everything on dry land that had the breath of life in its nostrils died. Every living thing on the face of the earth was wiped out; men and animals and the creatures that move along the ground and the birds of the air were wiped from the earth (Gen. 7:21–23).

What a scene of devastation and destruction! In subsequent scenes of God's judgments, not only were people affected but even plants and animals. When God destroyed Sodom and Gomorrah by raining down sulfur on them, he also destroyed "the vegetation in the land" (Gen. 19:25). In God's judgments on Egypt before the Exodus, all the livestock of the Egyptians died in one plague (Exod. 9:6). All creation was affected by the fall of Adam and Eve (Rom. 8:20–22), although to what extent is not made clear.[19] People have been given dominion over creation and are responsible for it. Consequently, the whole world, animals included, suffered in the judgment of the Flood. The increase in the waters and its churning in triumph was a reversal of God's blessing at creation when he filled the earth with birds, living creatures, and people (Gen. 1:22, 28). Now only death, destruction, and chaos were left.

Judgment came because God hates sin and rebellion against his authority. He will not stand for it, being a holy God. But God understood that judgment on humanity would not cure their sin or change their hearts (Gen. 6:5, 8:21). He preserved humanity so that his provision for taking the deserved judgment for sin would come through his incarnate Son (Isa. 53:4–6).

But people continue to go their own ways, rebelling against God's authority, becoming "filled with every kind of wickedness, evil, greed and depravity" (Rom. 1:29). Paul warned us, "The wrath of God is being revealed from heaven against all the godlessness and wickedness of men who suppress the truth by their wickedness" (Rom. 1:18). He went on to tell us why God is justified in his judgment: "We know that God's judgment against those who do such things is based on truth" (Rom. 2:2; cf. Ps. 96:13). All people are without excuse, for God has made plain to them since creation his "eternal power and divine nature" (Rom. 1:20). This can be seen in the intelligent design of the world around us. A greater power made us, and we are accountable to him.

We have seen that historical traditions of cultures throughout the world have accounts of a flood that destroyed humanity for their evil ways. But people today have forgotten what happened long ago that has been passed down for our warning. Most people have no fear of God but go about their business oblivious to the judgment they will face on death or the Lord's return. The apostle Peter reminded us of what these last days will be like.

First of all, you must understand that in the last days scoffers will come, scoffing and following their own evil desires. They will say, "Where is this 'coming' he promised? Ever since our fathers died, everything goes on as it has since the beginning of creation." But they deliberately forget that long ago by God's word the heavens existed and the earth was formed out of water and by water. By these waters also the world of that time was deluged and destroyed. By the same word the present heavens and earth are reserved for fire, being kept for the day of judgment and destruction of ungodly men. (2 Pet. 3:3–7)

Note that the scoffers "deliberately forget" the intervention of God in history when he brought his judgment. Of all events in history, the Flood shows that God is not indifferent to human affairs and that he cares about them. Flood traditions around the world showed that God has brought judgment in the past. Even those who do not know the Bible usually know about Noah and his ark, something they learned in early childhood. But most people continue in their sinful ways, rejecting the fact that someday they will be held accountable to God for their sins. The same word of God which created the universe also brought about the Flood and is preparing to destroy the earth with fire. Therefore, God warns us to flee the coming judgment on the ungodly by seeking refuge in Christ. Through him we may enter his kingdom ark and be saved from the flood of judgment.

We do not know when that day of judgment will come, but we must be ready. Jesus taught us to keep watch. He said,

"No one knows about that day or hour, not even the angels in heaven, nor the Son, but only the Father. As it was in the days of Noah, so it will be at the coming of the Son of Man. For in the days before the flood, people were eating and drinking, marrying and giving in marriage, up to the day Noah entered the ark; and they knew nothing about what would happen until the flood came and took them all away. That is how it will be at the coming of the Son of Man. Two men will be in the field; one will be taken and the other left. Two women will be grinding with a hand mill; one will be taken and the other left.

"Therefore keep watch, because you do not know on what day your Lord will come. . . . The Son of Man will come at an hour when you do not expect him." (Matt. 24:36–42, 44)

Are we ready and eagerly waiting for the Lord's return, or are we oblivious to it, like the people in Noah's day? Our only hope is to repent of our sins, trust in Christ to save us, and wait for his salvation in faith. The physical world will rejoice as will the righteous who eagerly wait for the Lord's coming judgment in righteousness, truth, and equity (Ps. 96:10–13; 98:7–9; Rom. 8:19).

SCRIPTURE READING:
Isaiah 54

Discussion Questions

1. What evidence do the Scriptures give as to whether the Flood was universal or local?
2. What difficulties do those who advocate a local Flood encounter?
3. What difficulties do those who advocate a universal Flood encounter?
4. What are the four major arguments Dr. Young makes against a young earth theory supported by a catastrophic flood?
5. Theologically, what if any difference does it make as to whether the Flood was local or universal?
6. How has God demonstrated his triumph over his enemies? What does that tell us about the power of God? Does that give you comfort or fear?
7. What are we reminded of in the gospel by the waters of judgment rising while the ark floated on top in safety?
8. Why must we not forget the judgment of the Flood? What can we anticipate yet to come?

Notes

1. Kenneth Barker, gen. ed., *The NIV Study Bible* (Grand Rapids: Zondervan, 1985), 15.

2. John C. Whitcomb Jr. and Henry M. Morris, *The Genesis Flood* (Philadelphia: Presbyterian and Reformed, 1963), 110–111.

3. Warren E. Leary, "Found: Possible Pre-Flood Artifacts," *New York Times,* September 13, 2000, international edition.

4. In Genesis 5:32, we are told Noah "became the father of Shem, Ham and Japheth." One might conclude that this is the order of their birth. But in Genesis 9:24 we see reference to Ham as the *youngest* son. Names are omitted in some genealogical lists, apparently deliberately. Compare 1 Chronicles 6:3–14 with Ezra 7:2. In 1 Chronicles 26:24 at the time of King David at least a four hundred-year gap appears between Shubael and his ancestor Gershom, the son of Moses. Also in Jesus' genealogy (Matt. 1:8), a couple of names are omitted that are listed in 1 Chronicles 3:11, 12. The purpose is to show that each of these people is in the right genealogical line, rather than demonstrating exact chronology. So if we take the genealogy of Genesis 5, 10, and 11 as chronology, we would have Adam, Enoch and Methuselah as contemporaries and all those listed after the Flood, including Noah, as still living when Abram was fifty years old. Also Shem, Salah, and Eber would have outlived Abraham. This does not appear to fit the context. Additionally, many of the names refer to nations rather than to individuals.

5. Derek Kidner, *Genesis,* vol. 1, *The Tyndale Old Testament Commentaries* (Downers Grove, Ill.: InterVarsity Press, 1967), 95. Evidence for Mesopotamian floods has been found at Ur, Shuruppak, and Kish.

6 .Francis A. Schaeffer, *Genesis in Space and Time: The Flow of Biblical History* (Downers Grove, Ill.: InterVarsity, 1972), 134, 135. Some other sources date the crossing of the Bering Straits to North America at 15,000 BC.

7. Davis A. Young, *The Biblical Flood* (Grand Rapids: Eerdmans, 1995), 242.

8. This argument is not too likely in light of physical evidence for human life from ancient times around the globe, much of it most likely prior to the Flood.

9. Walt Brown, *In the Beginning: Compelling Evidence for Creation and the Flood,* 7th ed. (Phoenix, Ariz.: Center for Scientific Creation, 2001), 41.

10. Ibid., 100–101.

11. Young, *The Biblical Flood,* 294–295. He describes the arguments of Wayne Ault, a Christian geochemist.

12. See Davis A. Young, *Creation and the Flood: An Alternative to Flood Geology and Theistic Evolution* (Grand Rapids: Baker, 1977).

13. See the writings of Meredith G. Kline, such as "Genesis," in *The New Bible Commentary,* eds. D. Guthrie and J. A. Motyer (Grand Rapids: Eerdmans, 1970).

14. Young, *Creation and the Flood*, 176–210.

15. Ibid., 196, 197.

16. However, one could argue that the Hebrew word here translated *pitch* primarily means "a covering" from which we get our English word *cover*. It is the same word used to express "atonement" (Exod. 29:36; 30:10; Lev. 23:27, 28). Therefore, the covering could be something other than pitch.

17. For example, biblical interpretation of the rising and setting of the sun viewed the earth as the center of the universe with the sun revolving around the earth before Galileo's and Copernicus's discoveries.

18. Donald Grey Barnhouse, *Genesis: A Devotional Exposition*, vol. 1 (Grand Rapids: Zondervan, 1970), 57.

19. There is debate between the neo-catastrophists and uniformitarians as to the effect of the Fall on creation. Uniformitarians say that the curse as a result of the Fall was only on humankind and the serpent but not on the earth. Therefore, there was no change in the laws of thermodynamics or in the eating habits of some animals from being herbivorous to carnivorous. If some animals were not carnivorous, others, such as mice and rabbits, would overpopulate the earth and destroy the vegetation. Death, except that of humankind, occurred before the Fall. They would also say that we cannot read Romans 8:21, 22 as saying anything specific about animals or death. Neo-catastrophists would say the opposite on all these points. See Davis A. Young, *Creation and the Flood*, 159–169, for an uniformitarian approach.

But God Remembered Noah

Genesis 7:24–8:14

24 The waters flooded the earth for a hundred and fifty days.

8 *But God remembered Noah and all the wild animals and the livestock that were with him in the ark, and he sent a wind over the earth, and the waters receded. 2 Now the springs of the deep and the floodgates of the heavens had been closed, and the rain had stopped falling from the sky. 3 The water receded steadily from the earth. At the end of the hundred and fifty days the water had gone down, 4 and on the seventeenth day of the seventh month the ark came to rest on the mountains of Ararat. 5 The waters continued to recede until the tenth month, and on the first day of the tenth month the tops of the mountains became visible.*

6 After forty days Noah opened the window he had made in the ark 7 and sent out a raven, and it kept flying back and forth until the water had dried up from the earth. 8 Then he sent out a dove to see if the water had receded from the surface of the ground. **9** *But the dove could find no place to set its feet because there was water over all the surface of the earth; so it returned to Noah in the ark. He reached out his hand and took the dove and brought it back to himself in the ark.* **10** *He waited seven more days and again sent out the dove from the ark.* **11** *When the dove returned to him in the evening, there in its beak was a freshly plucked olive leaf! Then Noah knew that the water had receded from the earth.* **12** *He waited seven more days and sent the dove out again, but this time it did not return to him.*

13 *By the first day of the first month of Noah's six hundred and first year, the water had dried up from the earth. Noah then removed the covering from the ark and saw that the surface of the ground was dry.* **14** *By the twenty-seventh day of the second month the earth was completely dry.*

A S BELIEVERS we look forward to our deliverance from suffering and persecution, although that time has not yet arrived. God is refining our faith through trials and testing. Yet the LORD remembers his people in a timely way to fulfill his covenant promises. As we wait for our final redemption, we find that the church has a mixture of both clean and unclean in its external form until the judgment day. In the meantime, we eagerly and patiently look forward to the re-created heavens and earth. Yet Noah and his family had to patiently wait for about a year to enter the new beginning of the re-created earth.

◦∾ Redemption in Remembrance

"The waters flooded the earth for a hundred and fifty days" (Gen. 7:24). This is five months of continual water flowing over the earth. Noah and his family were safe, but they were not yet saved. Moses then gave an account of the abatement of the Flood. Up to this point, it had focused on judgment. Now we come to God's redemption.

Many months went by without Noah hearing anything from the LORD. Did Noah complain about all those stinking animals he had to take care of? Did he complain of their confinement on the ark? Did he think God had forgotten him? Apparently, he did not. He waited patiently for the LORD to act.

"But God remembered Noah and all the wild animals and the livestock that were with him in the ark . . ." (Gen. 8:1). God's remembrance of Noah was based on his previous commitment to him, not just a mental recall, as if he had forgotten about him for the past 150 days. Previously, he told Noah, "I will establish my covenant with you" (Gen. 6:18). God keeps his covenant. The term *remembered* (זכר) used here in the context of God's covenant with Noah described one who was actively mindful of his commitments and who now carried them out.[1]

Similarly, when the Israelites cried out to the LORD during their slavery in Egypt, "God heard their groaning and he *remembered* his covenant with Abraham, with Isaac and with Jacob. So God looked on the Israelites and was concerned about them" (Exod. 2:24, 25, emphasis added). When Zechariah, father of John the Baptist, prophesied, he said, "He has raised up a horn of salvation for us . . . to *remember* his holy covenant, the oath he swore to our father Abraham" (Luke 1:69, 72, 73, emphasis added). He spoke of God's redemption coming in the birth of Jesus as the fulfillment of his covenant promises after four hundred years of silence.

Although God had been silent while Noah waited in the ark, now he remembered and expressed his loving concern and care for Noah. In remembering his people, God does so "with favor." We see this in Nehemiah's prayer: "Remember me with favor, O my God, for all I have done for these people" (Neh. 5:19; also see 13:31). God's remembrance "combines the ideas of faithful love and timely intervention." God moved toward the object of his memory.[2] He intervened on behalf of Noah to save him at just the right time. So what had been presented to Noah as God's covenantal purpose in chapter 6 was now being fulfilled in chapter 8 for his salvation.

If God had not remembered Noah, he would not be the same God who has revealed himself to us throughout Scripture as a faithful God who remembers his covenant promises forever. If Noah had been lost, how could God's promise to Eve be fulfilled that through her Seed would come one who would crush the head of Satan? But God knows and remembers those who are his. Paul told Timothy in the context of a warning about false teachers, "Nevertheless, God's solid foundation stands firm, sealed with this inscription: 'The Lord knows those who are his'" (2 Tim. 2:19). As Barnhouse notes, "If God had not remembered Noah, all that Noah would have lost would have been his soul, but God would have lost His honor."[3]

Not only did God remember Noah, but he also remembered "all the wild animals and the livestock that were with him in the ark" (8:1). Just as wicked humanity was destroyed in the Flood along with the brute beasts, so in preserving the elect family, God also showed his goodness to the animal kingdom. God's care for the animals in the ark reminds us of what Jesus said, "Are not two sparrows sold for a penny? Yet not one of them will fall to the ground apart from the will of your Father. . . . So don't be afraid; you are worth more than many sparrows" (Matt. 10:29, 31). Because God cares for even the most insignificant animals, he will certainly care for his own children whom he dearly loves.

The description of Noah's rescue from judgment foreshadows the redemption of Israel from Egypt through the Exodus. Numerous parallels may be drawn between them. God "remembered his covenant" with the Israelites' forefathers (Exod. 2:24) and "drove the sea back with a strong east wind and turned it into dry land" so that the Israelites could go through the Red Sea "on dry ground" (Exod. 14:21, 22). Similarly, "God remembered Noah" and all those in the ark, "sent a wind over the earth" (Gen. 8:1), and called them out onto dry ground (Gen. 8:13–15). As John Sailhamer says, "We must reckon with the fact that the author is deliberately recounting these various events in such a way to highlight their similarity. God's dealings in the past prefigure his work in the present and the future."[4] Knowing this to be true, we can have assurance that God will remember us, to whom he has given his covenant promises. Jesus has already suffered the judgment for us, so the wind of his Holy Spirit has moved in our hearts to seal us. He will bring us onto the dry ground of the Promised Land, where all things have been made new.

∼ A New Beginning

God "sent a wind over the earth, and the waters receded" (Gen. 8:1). In Psalm 104 the psalmist described the winds as personified agents of God's purposes when he said, "He makes winds his messengers" (v. 4). Some have thought that the wind after the Flood may have been warm, thus causing rapid evaporation. But as Ambrose comments, "In fact the wind had no power to dry the deluge. Otherwise the sea, which is moved every day by the winds, would become empty. How would the sea become empty because of the strength of the winds alone? . . . There is no doubt, therefore, that that deluge was subsided by the invisible power of the Spirit, not through the wind as such but through divine intervention."[5]

What is more significant about the wind is that it is the same Hebrew word which is translated as "Spirit" in Genesis 1:2. The wind calls to mind the creation account when "the earth was formless and empty, darkness was over the surface of the deep, and the Spirit of God was hovering over the waters" (Gen. 1:2). The wind introduced God's first re-creation out of chaos, thus renewing the earth out of the waters.

Following the action of the wind came a series of re-creative acts of God that parallel those of creation. In Genesis 8:2–5, we have the gathering of the water so that it receded, paralleling the separation of water on the earth from sky and seas from dry land (Gen. 1:6–10) in the creation account. As Noah sent out a raven and a dove from the ark, so God created the birds to fly in the sky (1:20–22). God caused the water to recede so that dry ground appeared and vegetation grew. This paralleled God's creation of the dry ground to produce vegetation in the creation account (1:9–12). As people and animals went out of the ark to procreate and fill the earth (8:16–19), so God had created the animals and humans on the sixth day to do the same (1:24–27). As Noah made a "sabbatical consecration of the creation kingdom in the ark to the Creator Lord"[6] (8:20–22), so God rested on the seventh day and made it holy (2:2, 3). Finally, God blessed Noah and his sons (9:1–3) as he had blessed man and woman when he had first created them in his image to multiply and have dominion over the earth (1:27–30).

Another form of literary parallelism is seen in the fiat–fulfillment format of the stanzas of the days of creation. That is, God spoke the word and created the world out of nothing. In the Flood account, fiat–fulfillment took the form of command-fulfillment (through Noah's obedience) in its first six sections. Fiat-fulfillment is also seen in the coming of the Flood, the prevailing of the waters for the destruction of life, and the passing of the wind over the earth to diminish the waters and rest the ark.

A conscious effort was made in the Flood account to parallel the creation account to signify a virtual re-creation of the earth. Two triads of three sections each have a unifying theme for each triad. The first triad has a unifying theme of entrance of the ark-kingdom into the judgment. The second triad's theme is reemergence of the ark-kingdom in the re-creation. The climatic middle section of the Flood account (A.B.A' structure) corresponds to the seventh section in the creation account (with an A.A'.B structure where A represents the forming on the first three days, A'. represents the filling on the second three days, while B. represents the Sabbath rest). A chiastic

arrangement may be seen in the correspondence between the two triads so that the first and the seventh, the second and the sixth, and
the third and the fifth sections are matching. This literary parallelism
made a division between the two worlds of the antediluvian heavens
and earth of old and the present heavens and earth. It also anticipated the act of re-creation of the new heavens and earth following
the judgment ordeal by fire described by Peter (2 Pet. 3:5–7). The
final coming of God's consummated kingdom will necessitate drastic measures of cosmic re-creation through a cataclysm of fire.[7]

⟶ Patient Waiting on the LORD

Noah and his family waited in the ark for one hundred and fifty days
before they saw God's deliverance begin. The account does not give
us any details of that time period. It was simply a period of waiting
on the LORD. The Israelites had to wait four hundred and thirty
years while they were slaves in Egypt before the LORD brought
about their deliverance (Exod. 12:40, 41). Then they had to wait
another forty years in the wilderness before their deliverance into
the Promised Land (Num. 14:33, 34). During each of these time
periods, Scripture is silent as to what happened between the beginning and the end. Now, too, we are to wait patiently for the Lord's
deliverance. Some day soon Jesus will return for our salvation.

In the seventh month, after the beginning of the Flood, the ark
rested on the mountains of Ararat. The kingdom of God exemplified by the ark-community of Noah and his family was brought to
a point of Sabbath consummation. The Hebrew term for resting of
the ark (נוח) used a play on the name of Noah, who was to bring
relief from toil (Gen. 5:29). It was a term used to describe God's
resting from creation (Exod. 20:11) and the glory–Spirit ("hand of
the LORD") resting on Mount Zion at the consummation-Sabbath
at the end of the age (Isa. 25:10). The Spirit of the LORD called
Israel to rest in the Sabbath-land of Canaan (Isa. 63:14). By the

Spirit ("wind," Gen. 8:1) bringing the ark to rest, we see the image of the microcosmic house of God. The ark was a replica of the Tabernacle and Temple, coming to share in the Sabbath of the glory-Spirit-temple of heaven. God's image bearers in the ark were now being perfected in his likeness by sharing in his Sabbath.

As believers, we too will rest from our trials, toil, and striving. Christ has done the work of making us into a new creation. We are not called to enter our own rest but his rest, since his work is completed. "Since the promise of entering his rest still stands, let us be careful that none of [us] be found to have fallen short of it. . . . Now we who have believed enter that rest" (Heb. 4:1, 3).

All those five months (cf. Gen. 7:11; 8:4), the ark floated securely without rudder or sails, directed by the providence of God into a safe haven. So, too, the church, although assaulted by wind, rain, and rising streams is safe on the firm foundation of the Rock of our salvation (Matt. 7:25). In having its faith purified as gold through the refining fire of trial, the church in the ark contained the hope of the new world.

The water continued to recede until two and a half months later ("the first day of the tenth month") when the tops of the mountains appeared. After a long wait of forty days, Noah sent out an unclean raven, which eats carrion. The raven continued to fly back and forth until it found dry land. It was not a messenger of anything good. Rather, by not returning, it symbolized those who have been cleansed by the waters of baptism but have not put off the black clothes of their old selves to live holy lives. Instead, as persons of the flesh, they follow the desires of this life, filling themselves on the putrid flesh of this judged world (cf. Matt. 13:22).

When Noah sent out a clean dove, it returned on the second try with an olive leaf in its beak. This was a good sign of the everlasting peace Noah and we now have with God. His wrath against sin has been appeased in judgment, which was borne by Christ on the cross. Ever since then, the olive branch has been a symbol of peace. The dove also was a sign that the Spirit brings a new creation in conforming us to the image of Christ. All this has been symbolized in our baptism as the dove of the Holy Spirit, seen in sign and symbol, fills us by God's grace. Through Noah's sending out the two birds, we see his waiting and hoping for signs of God's remembrance of him. As the dove brought a symbol of the new creation, so the dove's symbolism of the Holy Spirit, which came on Jesus at his baptism, brings us hope of our new creation in Christ and hope of eternal life. We believers are filled with the Spirit, giving us assurance of the hope for which we live. The Spirit enables us to wait on the Lord in hope.

"By the first day of the first month of Noah's six hundred and first year, the water had dried up from the earth" (Gen. 8:13). After ten and a half months of floodwaters, the water had receded by New Year's Day. The indication of the date was a formula signaling a new beginning for humankind.

But Noah continued to wait another eight weeks. He removed the cover of the ark, looked out, and saw that the ground was dry. "By the twenty-seventh day of the second month the earth was completely dry" (8:14). So it was a year and ten (some count eleven) days after the beginning of the Flood that the earth became completely dry again (see 7:11). (According to a lunar calendar, it would have been exactly one year.) Yet Noah waited until the LORD called him out before leaving the ark (8:15–17). He exercised self-discipline and patience as he waited for God's timing and word.[8] So, too, we are to wait in this earthly life, having seen the blessings of the kingdom of God in part but not yet experiencing it in its fullness until the end of the age.

Sometimes things are so bad that we may wonder whether it is worth waiting on the Lord. If we would only compromise in our stand for Jesus Christ, we could escape the suffering we are forced to endure. Such was the suffering of many pastors before and during the Cultural Revolution in China. One faithful pastor was Wong Ming-Dao. He was released from prison in January 1980 after twenty-three years at the age of almost eighty. Though weak in body, he was strong in spirit. He remained steadfast in the midst of unremitting pressures. He told how the words of the prophet Micah sustained him.[9]

> But as for me, I watch in hope for the LORD,
>   I wait for God my Savior;
>   my God will hear me. (Mic. 7:7)

What we see from the portrait "of Noah in the narrative is that of a righteous and faithful remnant patiently waiting for God's deliverance."[10] Every living thing was wiped out from the earth. "Only Noah was left, and those with him in the ark" (7:23). We are to wait on the LORD, as Isaiah was instructed to do when Israel turned away from their God. "I will wait for the LORD, who is hiding his face from the house of Jacob. I will put my trust in him" (Isa. 8:17). What does God promise to those who wait on him? "Those who hope in the LORD will renew their strength. They will soar on wings like eagles; they will run and not grow weary, they will walk and not be faint" (Isa. 40:31).

James gave us encouragement to be patient in waiting for the Lord's timing in the midst of our suffering.

> Be patient, then, brothers, until the Lord's coming. See how the farmer waits for the land to yield its valuable crop and how patient he is for the autumn and spring rains. You too, be patient and stand firm, because the Lord's coming is near. Don't grumble against each other, brothers, or you will be judged. The Judge is standing at the door!
>
> Brothers, as an example of patience in the face of suffering, take the prophets who spoke in the name of the Lord. As you know, we consider blessed those who have persevered. You have heard of Job's perseverance and have seen what the Lord finally brought about. The Lord is full of compassion and mercy. (James 5:7–11)

Yes, the LORD blessed Job greatly for his perseverance, more so than before his severe trials and suffering. So, too, God blessed Noah for his patience, righteousness, and faith through his long wait on the LORD. We also will be blessed if we persevere in waiting patiently for the Lord's salvation, remaining faithful to him until the end.

Knowing the reality of God's judgment from the history of the Flood, we ought to make sure we are ready to meet our Maker. Do we have peace with God through Jesus Christ, or are we still his enemy? If we are at peace with God, we have a covenant relationship with him. He will never forget his covenant with us, for it cost him the price of Jesus' death. As God remembered Noah, God will remember us. If he cared enough to save the animals, he will care enough to save us for we are so much more valuable than they are (Matt. 6:26). In saving us, God makes all things new for us. He gives us a new beginning. The past is forgotten and forgiven.

When God seems quiet, and we don't see any signs of Jesus' coming soon to deliver us from the evils of this world, we must wait patiently for him in faith. He is true to his Word. He will not fail to come to deliver us from evil and to bless us beyond all we can imagine. He will triumph gloriously over his enemies, and we will reign with him eternally. Hallelujah!

SCRIPTURE READING:

2 Peter 3

Discussion Questions

1. How does the wind blowing over the water give us hope for a new beginning?
2. Knowing that God remembered Noah and his covenant with him, how does that encourage us today?
3. What hope can we get from the parallelism of the re-creation after the Flood with creation? Could we have a new beginning?

4. As the ark rested on the mountains, what rest does that picture for God's people? How do we enter that rest?

5. What contrasting symbolism may be found in the raven and the dove that were sent out from the ark?

6. As Noah patiently waited for about a year in the ark before coming out to a new beginning, how can we imitate his patience in seeing the Lord's renewal of all things?

Notes

1. This remembrance by our covenant-keeping God is in contrast to the remembrance, *zhikr*, done by Sufi Muslims through rapid repetition of one of the names of Allah, thus seeking to perceive the oneness of all being by the practitioner coming to a state of self-hypnosis.

2. Derek Kidner, *Genesis,* vol. 1 of *The Tyndale Old Testament Commentaries* (Downers Grove, Ill.: InterVarsity, 1967), 92.

3. Donald Grey Barnhouse, *Genesis: A Devotional Exposition*, vol. 1 (Grand Rapids: Zondervan, 1970), 58.

4. John Sailhamer, "Genesis," in vol. 2 of *The Expositor's Bible Commentary*, ed. Frank E. Gaebelein (Grand Rapids: Zondervan, 1990), 89.

5. Andrew Louth, ed., *Genesis 1–11*, OT vol. 1 of *Ancient Christian Commentary on Scripture* (Downers Grove, Ill.: InterVarsity, 2001), 143.

6. Meredith G. Kline, *Kingdom Prologue* (Overland Park, Kans.: Two Age Press, 2000), 229.

7. Ibid., 220–225.

8. Kidner, *Genesis*, 92.

9. Wong Ming-Dao, preface and introduction to *A Stone Made Smooth* (Southampton, Hants, U.K.: Mayflower, 1981).

10. John Sailhamer, "Genesis," 90.

Noah Came Out and Worshiped

Genesis 8:15–22

15 *Then God said to Noah,* **16** *"Come out of the ark, you and your wife and your sons and their wives.* **17** *Bring out every kind of living creature that is with you—the birds, the animals, and all the creatures that move along the ground—so they can multiply on the earth and be fruitful and increase in number upon it."*

18 *So Noah came out, together with his sons and his wife and his sons' wives.* **19** *All the animals and all the creatures that move along the ground and all the birds—everything that moves on the earth—came out of the ark, one kind after another.*

20 *Then Noah built an altar to the* LORD *and, taking some of all the clean animals and clean birds, he sacrificed burnt offerings on it.* **21** *The* LORD *smelled the pleasing aroma and said in his heart: "Never again will I curse the ground*

*because of man, even though every inclination of his heart is
evil from childhood. And never again will I destroy all living
creatures, as I have done.*

22 *"As long as the earth endures,
    seedtime and harvest,
    cold and heat,
    summer and winter,
    day and night
    will never cease."*

G OD TOLD NOAH and his family to come out of the ark
as a sign of his mercy and grace to live in newness of life.
This deliverance from death is symbolic of our baptism and
resurrection life. Having been saved from God's judgment, Noah
worshiped his Creator with thanks. He made a Sabbath consecration
of the creation to the Creator-King. In grace the LORD responded to
Noah's worship with a covenant promise despite knowing that people's thoughts were evil from childhood. Thus, the generations since
Noah by common grace have enjoyed the seasons of the year, bringing our harvests.

∽ Come Out of the Ark

"Then God said to Noah, 'Come out of the ark, you and your wife
and your sons and their wives'" (Gen. 8:15).

Noah's coming out of the ark was leaving entombment in death
for a resurrection life. His coming out of the watery grave into the
re-created world was a type of our resurrection and renewed life.
Symbolically, Noah died to sin, leaving his sins behind and walking
into a new creation by faith. God's deliverance of Noah and his
family in the ark was simply a preliminary step to his real earthly

salvation—walking into a new creation. Noah stepped out into a new world washed clean of all defilement. He also became head of a new race with a new beginning.

Noah's coming out of the ark was described in a pattern similar to that of creation, although in a condensed form. We note the similarity with the creation account, particularly when God instructed Noah concerning the animals saying, "So they can multiply on the earth and be fruitful and increase in number upon it" (Gen. 8:17; cf. Gen. 1:22). Here was a return to creation "in the beginning." It was with this restored new creation that a covenant was established.

Similar to the description of the entry into the ark, the sentence structure is epic repetition in describing the exit from the ark. The purpose for repeating both in the conversation between God and Noah and then in the description of what happened when Noah came out "with his sons and his wife and his sons' wives" and "all the animals and all the creatures that move along the ground and all the birds" is "to slow down the pace of the narrative. It holds the picture a little longer and enforces it on the mind."[1] Through the repetition, we grasp the importance of what happened redemptively.

A striking parallel occurs between the call of Noah out of the ark (8:15–20) and the call of Abram out of Ur (12:1–7). John Sailhamer delineates these as follows:

Genesis 8:15–20

    a. "Then God said to Noah" (8:15)
    b. "Come out of the ark" (8:16).
    c. "So Noah came out" (8:18).
    d. "Then Noah built an altar to the LORD" (8:20).
    e. "Then God blessed Noah" (9:1).
    f. " 'Be fruitful and increase' " (9:1).
    g. " 'I now establish my covenant with you and with your descendants' " (9:9).

Genesis 12:1–7

a. "The LORD had said to Abram" (12:1).

b. " 'Leave your country' " (12:1).

c. "So Abram left" (12:4).

d. "So [Abram] built an altar there to the LORD" (12:7).

e. " 'And I [God] will bless you' " (12:2).

f. " 'I will make you into a great nation' " (12:2).

g. " 'To your offspring, I will give this land' " (12:7).

"Both Noah and Abraham represent new beginnings in the course of events recorded in Genesis. Both are marked by God's promise of blessing and his gift of the covenant."[2] The call of Noah indicates the importance of his place in the history of God's redemption of humankind. As Abraham was the friend of God and the father of our faith, so Noah walked with God and was an example of righteousness through faith.

After Noah and his family waited patiently in the ark for just over a year, "God said to Noah, 'Come out of the ark' " (Gen. 8:15). Since Noah and his family's deliverance through the Flood was portrayed in the New Testament as a type of the Christian's baptism (1 Pet. 3:20–21), we may see their coming out of the ark as the emergence from the waters of death to new life.[3] Jesus said, " 'a time is coming when all who are in their graves will hear [the Son of God's] voice and come out' " (John 5:28, 29). After Jesus' friend Lazarus had been in the tomb for four days, Jesus visited Lazarus' sisters Mary and Martha.

> Then Jesus said, "Did I not tell you that if you believed, you would see the glory of God?" . . .
>
> Jesus called in a loud voice, "Lazarus, *come out!*" The dead man *came out,* his hands and feet wrapped with strips of linen, and a cloth around his face.
>
> Jesus said to them, "Take off the grave clothes and let him go." (John 11:40, 43, 44, emphasis added)

Here is a picture of what it means to "come out" of death into life. Of course, Noah and his family, as well as Lazarus, eventually died physically. But what happened to bring them from death to life helps us see how we are saved out of spiritual death and brought into eternal life. As symbolized in our baptism, we have died to sin and can no longer live in it. Our old lives of sin have undergone the waters of judgment. As Paul wrote, "Or don't you know that all of us who were baptized into Christ Jesus were baptized into his death? We were therefore buried with him through baptism into death in order that, just as Christ was raised from the dead through the glory of the Father, we too may live a new life" (Rom. 6:3, 4). In being called out of the ark in a symbolic sense, Noah and his family passed through the waters of judgment into a new creation. Paul continued, "If we have been united with him like this in his death, we will certainly also be united with him in his resurrection" (v. 5). In being united with Christ in his resurrection, prefigured in Noah's coming out of the ark, we see a prefigured new humanity that has overcome evil. This humanity has a close relationship with God because of the covenant love pledged by God toward his elect. Since Jesus has overcome the world, we too can overcome it by the power of the Holy Spirit who lives within us and has marked us with his seal.

Worship the LORD

This portion of the Flood narrative (Gen. 8:20–22) deals with the Sabbath consecration of the creation-kingdom in the ark to the Creator LORD on the consummation of entering God's rest. The Sabbath rest is a type of our rest from our labors by entering God's rest by his grace. To enter God's rest is to enter his kingdom. Those who believe enter that rest (Heb. 4:3). Our final celebration of entering our Sabbath rest will be in the future age, which he invites us to share (Heb. 4:9–11).

Noah assumed the priestly office by offering clean animals as burnt offerings to consecrate him and his family to the LORD. They acknowledged as servant-kings in the kingdom-house of the ark that their Vindicator was the King of kings. This consecration of the ark-kingdom reminds us of the priestly role of the royal Son, who on his return in glory, will turn the consummated kingdom over to God the Father. The Father will "put everything under Christ. When he has done this, then the Son himself will be made subject to him who put everything under him, so that God may be all in all" (1 Cor. 15:27, 28). Thus, in the new creation, Noah consecrated the kingdom that came through the judgment ordeal victoriously to the service of its Redeemer-King.

Worship of the Lord is one of the unique things about men and women that separates them from the animal world. We were made to worship God. When we don't know the true and living God, we invent some god of our own imaginations to worship because we know a higher power over us must be worshiped. Noah knew who the true God was. He had such a close relationship with him that the Lord even spoke to him. In the context of this relationship, Noah built an altar to worship him.

If we look at the events before the Flood and the fact that only Noah and his family survived, we assume they were grateful that they were still alive. So their pleasing burnt sacrifices in worship to God were certainly offered with thanksgiving. We could say that this was the beginning of our Thanksgiving Day tradition. It was to "make God's praise to be glorious."[4] Similarly the church, after having gone through many trials, sufferings, and opposition, will give eternal thanksgiving to God in the heavenly Zion where we will continually sing our Savior's praises with joy (Isa. 35:10; 51:3, 11). Noah and his family had entered the eternal kingdom (figuratively in the ark) that cannot be shaken, having passed through the destructive Flood. The author of Hebrews told us how we are to approach God in worship. "Therefore, since we are receiving a kingdom that cannot be shaken, let us *be thankful,* and so worship God acceptably with reverence and awe, for our 'God is a consuming fire' " (Heb. 12:28, 29, emphasis added).

Additionally, Noah's offering was a sacrifice of dedication of him and his family to the service of God. But ultimately, it was one of propitiation and atonement for sin. Propitiation means the removal of the wrath of God against sin by the offering of a gift. Atonement is bringing together in unity those who have been estranged, so sinners are reconciled with our holy God. Only in this way can we sinners approach God in worship.

This is the first place in Genesis where an altar is mentioned, although we are told of the sacrifices of Cain and Abel in chapter 4. An altar means "the place of slaughter." Bloody animal sacrifices were made to restore right relationships with our holy God. Noah built an altar to the LORD, to Yahweh, the covenant-keeping God. He called on the LORD by his personal name, which emphasizes his role as Redeemer and the God of the covenant. He was mindful of the LORD's faithfulness to his covenant promises (6:18), so he offered sacrifices out of thanksgiving. But being a man who walked with God, he also realized his own sinfulness. He knew he needed to have atonement for his sins and those of his family.

It is not clear from the passage as to how Noah knew what a clean or unclean animal was. It may have been through a special revelation from God. It must have been the same as was defined under Mosaic Law in Leviticus 11 and Deuteronomy 14. Clean animals were those that had split hooves completely divided and that chewed the cud, such as cows, sheep, goats, and deer. Clean birds were doves and pigeons (Lev. 1:14). Unclean birds were eagles, hawks, owls, vultures, storks, and herons. Unclean animals, such as animals that walk on their four paws, weasels, rats, lizards, geckos, flying insects (except those with jointed legs for hopping) were not to be eaten or sacrificed because God's people were holy to the LORD (Lev. 11:44, 45; Deut. 14:21). It was a means of distinguishing them from the rest of the world that was outside God's covenant community. They were set apart to be holy just as God is holy and pure.

A large number of clean animals came out of the ark, for Noah took in seven pairs of each clean animal and bird. Even if he sacrificed only one of each kind, he would have offered a great many. But who would have a more appropriate occasion to give thanks than Noah? It was a most solemn occasion of not only giving thanks, but also the sacrifices covered the sins of Noah and his family. They were offered to the LORD, our only hope in light of our depraved, sinful condition. They were offered in anticipation of the coming Seed of Eve who would crush Satan's head. Although God required such sacrifices, "it is impossible for the blood of bulls and goats to take away sins" but "we have been made holy through the sacrifice of the body of Jesus Christ once for all" (Heb. 10:4, 10). In faith Noah looked forward to God's eternal salvation represented through the animal sacrifices he made.

"The LORD smelled the pleasing aroma and said in his heart: 'Never again will I curse the ground because of man' " (Gen. 8:21). The burning sacrifices were pleasing to the LORD, as all rightful worship to him does. Other words that describe the pleasing aroma to the LORD are *restful, soothing,* or *pleasant.* The LORD takes delight in his children's worship, and he received satisfaction from the sacrifice. In offering sacrifices, the worshiper typified the idea of self-consecration as the offerings went completely up to the LORD in fire.[5] The pleasing offerings at the altar were a consecration of the kingdom in the ark that had now been consummated in redemptive re-creation. Those in the ark now confessed their subjection to the sovereign rule of God. The sacrifices were pleasing to the LORD because he was looking ahead to the sacrifice of Christ at Calvary for sinners. Christ gave his life as a sacrifice for us, turning away the wrath of God and interceding on our behalf before the Father. Through his death, we have atonement and propitiation accomplished for us with God. Only Christ is acceptable to his Father, so we are only accepted through him. Jesus' death was the Father's will and pleased him. "Christ loved us and gave himself up for us as a fragrant offering and sacrifice to God" (Eph. 5:2). Therefore, we no longer have to offer animal sacrifices.

As Christians we are to offer our whole lives as living sacrifices consecrated to the LORD. Paul wrote, "Therefore, I urge you, brothers, in view of God's mercy, to offer your bodies as living sacrifices, holy and pleasing to God—this is your spiritual act of worship" (Rom. 12:1). As Christ lives in us, he "spreads everywhere the fragrance of the knowledge of him. For we are to God the aroma of Christ among those who are being saved and those who are perishing. To the one we are the smell of death; to the other, the fragrance of life" (2 Cor. 2:14–16). Our imitation of Christ in living a life of love is a fragrant offering and sacrifice to God (Eph. 5:1, 2). Even as we give of our material wealth to the Lord's work, it is a pleasing sacrifice to him. As Paul thanked the Philippians for their gifts, he said, "They are a fragrant offering, an acceptable sacrifice, pleasing to God" (Phil. 4:18). When we dedicate our lives to the Lord's service, may it be a sweet aroma of worship pleasing to him. In that way, whether we eat or drink or whatever we do, it will all be done for the glory of God (1 Cor. 10:31).

The LORD's resolve never to curse the ground or destroy all living creatures again because of people was made in response to the heartfelt prayer of Noah as he worshiped. We are reminded of what James told us, "The prayer of a righteous man is powerful and effective" (James 5:16). Noah, a man who walked with God, offered powerful prayers that brought blessing to the human race.

∾ Original Sin

"The LORD smelled the pleasing aroma and said in his heart: 'Never again will I curse the ground because of man, even though every inclination of his heart is evil from childhood. And never again will I destroy all living creatures, as I have done' " (Gen. 8:21).

The language of the declaration that the LORD's wrath was turned aside by the pleasing aroma of sacrifices provides an alternative to God's earlier judicial decree before the Flood. Then the account said,

> The LORD saw how great man's wickedness on the earth had become, and that every inclination of the thoughts of his heart was only evil all the time. The LORD was grieved that he had made man on the earth, and his heart was filled with pain. So the LORD said, "I will wipe mankind, whom I have created, from the face of the earth—men and animals, and creatures that move along the ground, and birds of the air—for I am grieved that I have made them." (Gen. 6:5–7)

Before the Flood, the LORD's heart was filled with pain, and he grieved over humankind. Now the LORD's heart determined from the pleasing aroma to never destroy people and animals by flood again. He also decided to never curse the ground again. His curse on the ground was by means of the Flood, using nature to curse people. But this did not change nature itself. It did not change the curse on the ground due to Adam's sin, so production would continue to be only through painful toil, and it would still produce thorns and thistles (Gen. 3:17–19). It may be that God was promising not to bring a curse upon a curse, as when he had cursed Cain, and the ground produced nothing for him (Gen. 4:11–12).

But note that people's spiritual condition was still the same after the Flood as before. Before the Flood a person was described as "every inclination of the thoughts of his heart was only evil all the time" (Gen. 6:5). Now God said, "Every inclination of his heart is evil from childhood" (Gen. 8:21). This evil disposition was due to what is called original sin. That is, all people are sinful from conception and birth due to their inherited natures passed on from the fall of Adam. As King David confessed, "Surely I was sinful at birth, sinful from the time my mother conceived me" (Ps. 51:5). Job asked, " 'Who can bring what is pure from the impure? No one!' " (Job 14:4). His friend Eliphaz asked, " 'What is man, that he could be pure, or one born of woman, that he could be righteous?' " (Job 15:14). His other friend Bildad also asked, " 'How then can a man be righteous before God? How can one born of woman be pure?' " (Job 25:4).

Adam held a federal or representative headship of the human race (Rom. 5:12–19). So when Adam fell into sin, he brought universal ruin to all humanity. When Adam fell, we fell with him. The evidence for this is seen in every child. No one needs to teach a young child to be selfish, strong-willed, and disobedient. Evil tendencies are not just picked up from others and the environment, but they come from our own evil hearts. As Jesus taught, " 'What comes out of a man is what makes him "unclean." For from within, out of men's hearts, come evil thoughts, sexual immorality, theft, murder, adultery, greed, malice, deceit, lewdness, envy, slander, arrogance and folly. All these evils come from inside and make a man "unclean" ' " (Mark 7:20–23).

The new field of evolutionary psychology is now discovering that human nature has a dark side that the Scriptures have taught us all along as original sin. It has found that all types of ordinary people, both rich and poor, educated and uneducated, church-affiliated and atheists, have the capacity to be genocidal executioners as has been witnessed in the over sixty million people who were victims of genocide in the twentieth century. We all have the capacity of committing extraordinary evil. James Waller says this calls for structuring "a society in which the gross exercise of human evil is constrained." Understanding our own capacity for evil and how we can curb that capacity with moral development will provide safeguards against future expressions of depravity.[6] As we will see shortly, the institution of the state is one means of restraining humanity's inherent evil.

The continuance of evil after the Flood was like an avalanche that nothing could stop. Jeremiah described our hearts like this: "The heart is deceitful above all things, and desperately sick; who can understand it?" (Jer. 17:9 ESV). The heart represents one's character, mind, and will. Our perverse hearts affect all our choices and relationships. As we will see in Genesis 9, although Noah was a righteous man who walked with God, he too fell into sin, as did his descendants. Knowing what evil hearts we have, we must constantly guard them. As Proverbs says, "Above all else, guard your heart, for it is the wellspring of life" (Prov. 4:23). Jesus came to give us transplanted hearts. He will exchange our hearts of stone for hearts of flesh (Ezek. 36:26). We will then respond to the voice of our Lord and follow him.

∾ Never Again

In correspondence to our corrupt and evil hearts is the holy, just, fierce wrath of God, which was demonstrated in the Flood. However, despite the evil in men and women's hearts, God has extended his grace to us in restraining his wrath in judgment. The LORD "said in his heart: 'Never again will I curse the ground because of man. . . . And never again will I destroy all living creatures, as I have done'" (Gen. 8:21). "Von Rad speaks of a voluntary self-limitation of His punishing holiness, as the light of grace breaking through the darkness of wrath."[7] Church father Ambrose saw it this way: "Therefore God punished so that we might fear and forgave so that we might be preserved. He punished once in order to give an example that would have raised fear, but he forgave for the future, so that the bitterness of sin would not have prevailed."[8] The object lesson for humanity was already given. It did not need to be repeated. Human nature had not changed. If there had been a curse on the ground for every sin of humanity, it would be an unending curse. In a way similar to the curse and judgment of the Flood being a onetime event, so the sacrifice of Jesus at the cross to take our curse and judgment was a onetime event. Jesus never needs to die again for sin (Heb. 10:10, 14) nor does anyone else for that matter. Since Christ has already paid our debt, God cannot seek to collect it a second time. Jesus said, "It is finished" (John 19:30).

God's special grace in his redemptive work in the lives of Noah and his family led to the blessings of common grace for the whole world. Similarly today, as Christians live for Christ, the common-grace blessings of God are extended throughout the culture in honesty, integrity, hard work, and family unity. In his covenant with Noah, God promised to continue the days, nights, and seasons of each year perpetually as long as the earth lasts. It was part of his covenant commitment to never destroy the earth again by flood (Gen. 9:11). He promised a uniformity of the laws of nature, not to be interrupted as in the Flood. God made the earth a protectorate of heaven until the final day of judgment. He determined to preserve the earth until our ultimate deliverance from sin. God alone guarantees that the covenant promises will be kept. He said,

> "As long as the earth endures,
> seedtime and harvest,
> cold and heat,
> summer and winter,
> day and night
> will never cease." (Gen. 8:22)

As the psalmist Asaph lamented the sense that the LORD had abandoned his people, he reminded the LORD of how he brought salvation on the earth, the days, and the seasons.

The day is yours, and yours also the night;
    you established the sun and moon.
It was you who set all the boundaries of the earth;
    you made both summer and winter. (Ps. 74:16, 17)

Here we recall the covenant promise made after the Flood. Because God is faithful to his covenant promises, we know we can rely on him at all times. He provides for our needs year after year just as he brings the changes to the seasons. These are blessings from God that we ought not to take for granted.

We see in this passage what we must do in coming to God and receiving his grace. First, there is nothing that we can do to receive his grace. It is unmerited favor freely given. We simply receive it as a gift and grow in it. Of course, from our human perspectives, we must seek the LORD with all our hearts (Isa. 55:6). However, the LORD finds us and draws us to himself (Isa. 65:1; John 6:37, 44, 65).

God chose to bless Noah and his family "before the beginning of time" (2 Tim. 1:9). He called them out of the ark after saving them from the Flood. They were called out to worship the LORD of creation. But God has provided us with the pattern for worshiping him. We cannot worship God just anyway we please. When we worship him rightly, he is pleased and blesses us for it. This is why Abel's worship was acceptable to the LORD while Cain's was not. In worshiping God, we must come before him as acknowledged sinners in need of redemption. We see that a holy blood sacrifice was necessary for our propitiation. We were purchased for God by the atonement of Jesus Christ, "the Lamb of God, who takes away the sin of the world" (John 1:29). In faith we look back to the perfect sacrifice of Jesus Christ on the cross for our sin. Noah looked forward in faith to that sacrifice of "the Lamb that was slain from the creation of the world" (Rev. 13:8). When we come to God in this way, through the perfect, finished work of Jesus Christ, we know we have an eternal relationship with him. So although we are great sinners, our sins are forgiven and covered, and we shall never perish. Hallelujah! Rejoice!

SCRIPTURE READING:
1 CHRONICLES 16:8–36

Discussion Questions

1. What is the spiritual significance of Noah's coming out of the ark?
2. What pleases God in our worship? How does he respond to it?
3. What is the spiritual condition of all people from birth?
4. How does our depravity express itself in society? What must happen to restrain evil?
5. How does the radical nature of humanity's sinfulness affect our ability to relate to God?
6. How does the LORD's promise never again to curse the ground relate to Jesus' death?
7. What signs of common grace has God extended to the whole world?
8. How has God blessed us despite our sins?

Notes

1. Francis I. Andersen, *Sentence in Biblical Hebrew* (New York: Walter De Gruyter, 1974), 40 as quoted by Sailhamer, "Genesis," 91.

2. Ibid., 91.

3. R. C. Sproul, ed., *New Geneva Study Bible* (Nashville: Thomas Nelson, 1995), 22.

4. Philip Graham Ryken, *My Father's World: Meditations on Christianity and Culture* (Phillipsburg, N.J.: Presbyterian and Reformed, 2002), 199, 201.

5. H. C. Leupold, *Exposition of Genesis*, vol. 1 (Grand Rapids: Baker, 1942), 322–323.

6. James E. Waller, "Deliver Us from Evil: Human Nature and Genocide," *Gordon College Stillpoint* (summer 2003): 11–13.

7. Berkouwer, *Man: The Image of God*, 140.

8. Andrew Louth, ed., *Genesis 1–11*, OT vol. 1 of *Ancient Christian Commentary on Scripture* (Downers Grove, Ill.: InterVarsity, 2001), 150.

A Renewed Mandate

Genesis 9:1–4

1 *Then God blessed Noah and his sons, saying to them, "Be fruitful and increase in number and fill the earth.* **2** *The fear and dread of you will fall upon all the beasts of the earth and all the birds of the air, upon every creature that moves along the ground, and upon all the fish of the sea; they are given into your hands.* **3** *Everything that lives and moves will be food for you. Just as I gave you the green plants, I now give you everything.*

4 *"But you must not eat meat that has its lifeblood still in it."*

GOD BLESSED humankind again after the Flood, recommissioning them to his kingdom agenda of filling and ruling the earth. From this middle section of the covenant given in the re-created world (Gen. 9:1–7), the common grace world order of the effects of the curse (Gen. 3:16–19; 4:15) continue in the new world but were stated in a more positive way. This was a strong indication that the covenant of Genesis 8:20—9:17 was a common-grace covenant. It should not be confused with the series of redemptive covenants God made with his elect people. Through his covenant with Noah and the earth, he revealed both his law and grace. His law related to the sanctity of life, and his grace related to his promise to never again destroy the earth by flood. This latter aspect will be looked at in two studies later. But as a whole, the scene after the Flood was more ominous concerning humankind's future. The scene was darkened by sin. Yes, people were still made in God's image and ruled over his creation as his viceroys, but now people were feared by the animals that became their food, and spreading violence was anticipated over the world.[1]

~ Fill the Earth

"God blessed Noah and his sons" (Gen. 9:1), renewing the original blessing given to man and woman after their creation (Gen. 1:28; also 5:2). At that time God said, "Be fruitful and increase in number; fill the earth and subdue it." So a second benediction was given to humankind. "God blessed Noah and his sons, saying to them, 'Be fruitful and increase in number and fill the earth' " (Gen. 9:1). Then after giving the command that we should not eat meat with its lifeblood still in it nor should we murder, God repeated the benediction given in the initial blessing. "As for you, be fruitful and increase in number; multiply on the earth and increase upon it" (Gen. 9:7). By beginning (v. 1) and ending (v. 7) this section, using a concentric style around humanity's function of dominion over the animals (vv. 2–4) and judicial authority given to the institution of the state, we see the great importance given to the family. With the assignment of filling the earth, the family has first and last place with the role of the state being secondary. So God reminds us that our primary cultural purpose is to reproduce and fill the earth with the image of God.

As a spiritual being in covenantal relationship with our Creator and made in his image, we are morally responsible for our actions and obligated to seek the good. As God's representative we are called to have dominion in his name, bringing the whole world to fruition and fulfillment. His trust to us is that we rule over all for his sake. This means we are to re-create, to re-produce, and to mould creation to God's will. This includes functioning in truth with power, to form artistically, and to seek harmony and beauty.[2]

The genealogies of Genesis indicate the reproductive fruitfulness fulfillment of God's blessing. As a common grace blessing, the reproductive sense of being fruitful, as opposed to meaning spiritual fruitfulness, has most relevance here. This is emphasized with the repeated similes of *fruitful, increase, fill,* and *multiply* (Gen. 9:1, 7). Implicit in this directive is that marriage and labor will continue as in the creation ordinance. They are good institutions given to people from the beginning, which ought not to be denigrated, lest the human race fail to fulfill its mandate. In multiplying and filling the earth, we are fulfilling God's purposes for glorifying his name throughout the world. As the pinnacle of God's creation, we are made in his image. Therefore, we can have a loving relationship with God through our mutual communication. As millions of people from every race, nation, tribe, and clan live for his glory, it brings pleasure to the heart of God.

People, many people, are on the heart of God—especially those whom he loved and for whom Christ died before the creation of the world (Eph. 1:4, 5). In the past thirty years or more, there has been much propaganda in the American media, in the United Nations, and in certain countries, particularly China, that we must have zero population growth. Much of the abortion industry's propaganda is based on this premise. But most of the zero population growth premises are based on faulty reasoning, incomplete facts, and lack of supporting data. Based on population figures from 1970, most of the world's land had less than two inhabitants per square mile. Less than 25 percent had 25 people per square mile. Five percent had over 250 people per square mile. By contrast, the average built-up suburb in America has about ten thousand inhabitants per square mile.[3] Between 1960 and 2000, the world's population doubled. But global population growth peaked around 1970, with a steady decline since then. This is due to smaller family sizes and the growing global AIDS crisis, especially in Africa.[4] Europe now has a birth rate of only 1.5 children per woman, with an expected decline in population of 70 million by 2050.[5] In the United States a record number of women between ages 15 to 44 are childless, with the rate of those foregoing or postponing motherhood rising nearly 10 percent between 1990 and 2002. Many couples have decided not to have children simply because "they don't want to alter the lifestyle they enjoy."[6]

As most people today are crowded into large cities, many assume that the whole world is like that. But you can drive for hours in the western United States, in Central Asia, or in the Argentine pampas and hardly see a single person off the highway. If everyone in the world lived in the United States, it would be about as crowded as New Jersey.[7] As Mother Teresa has said, "How can there be too many children? That's like saying there are too many flowers."

Countries suffer from starvation due primarily to war, government-enforced mismanagement, and sometimes drought or a combination of these causes. Even a country like India is less densely crowded than New Jersey, which is called the "Garden State" with large tracts of rural areas.[8] India produces more food than it can use, so it has warehouses filled with food that is rotting in puddles of water. New farming techniques and seed have greatly increased production in recent decades. But lack of concern for the poor leaves millions to go hungry.

In countries that make zero population growth a matter of policy, they have enforced the worst form of tyranny imaginable. We have seen this happening for the past couple of decades in China. People are sterilized against their wishes, and abortions are enforced, even right up to the time of normal delivery. Born children are abandoned and killed, especially girls, while others of the right sex are stolen and sold to childless families. Families with more than one child are heavily taxed into abject poverty by specialized taxes bearing no relation to income, ability to pay, or services offered by the government. Many Chinese counties charge a "social compensation fee" of two or three times a family's annual income to couples who exceed the limit of the one-child policy.[9] Guangdong, China, has now increased the fine to eight times a family's annual income.

Throughout history, an increase in population in a country has meant improvements in the quality of life, while stagnation or decline has brought disaster.[10] A declining population leads to human, social, and economic crises. In order to avoid a potentially explosive situation in Europe with its low birth rate, some countries are actually paying couples to have children. Why is it throughout the developing world that people are fleeing the countryside to go to the cities? It is because in the crowded cities the quality of life is usually much better, even if it is in a shantytown.

During the eight years of Bill Clinton's presidency, the American population increased by about 33 million people. This was a contributing factor to the booming economy the country had at that time. A higher birth rate (although only at about replacement level of 2.1 births per woman) and particularly higher immigration with an aging population has created more demand for products and services and thus many new jobs.

As we act within the mandate given to us by God to fill and rule the earth, we will be blessed and will fulfill God's plan for the families of the earth. Only God knows at what point he will decide the earth has been filled enough, and has been "filled with the knowledge of the glory of the LORD, as the waters cover the sea" (Hab. 2:14; cf. Isa. 11:9). I am not saying that birth control is immoral, as does the Roman Catholic Church. A couple should have as many children as they believe they can afford to raise. Children are a real blessing from

God, and any child that is conceived should have the full right to live to adulthood, or at least, until the Lord allows their life to come to an end. We don't have the right to take any person's life if we feel it is not convenient or useful, even that of the unborn (Ps. 139:13–16; Jer. 1:5).

Although as Christians we are living in the last days before Christ's return, we should continue to fulfill God's mandate of blessing our Creator through marriage and family. As Jeremiah wrote the exiles in Babylon, "Marry and have sons and daughters; find wives for your sons and give your daughters in marriage, so that they too may have sons and daughters. Increase in number there; do not decrease" (Jer. 29:6). This instruction was in the context of the LORD's direction to pray for and seek the peace and prosperity of an enemy city. In the same way, Christian families can bring peace and prosperity to the crooked and depraved cities in which they live as they "shine like stars in the universe as [they] hold out the word of life" (Phil. 2:15, 16).

⌇ Dominion over All Creatures

When Noah entered the renewed world, God gave him new instructions for his regency on the earth. God further developed the mandate given to Adam and Eve on the sixth day of creation concerning dominion.

Fear and Dread of You

"The fear and dread of you will fall upon all the beasts of the earth and all the birds of the air, upon every creature that moves along the ground, and upon all the fish of the sea; they are given into your hands" (Gen. 9:2).

God declared that men and women should have the dignity of covenantal lordship over the animals. This mandate was a further development of the commission given them to rule over creation when God said, "Rule over the fish of the sea and the birds of the air and over every living creature that moves on the ground" (Gen. 1:28). Some think that the fear of humans was already present in animals before this time. However, animals' lack of fear prior to the Flood may have contributed to Noah's ability to gather them into the ark and for Adam to name them as they came to him (Gen. 2:19, 20). But when God gave people permission to eat animals, they had reason to fear humans. And people were given some measure of protection because of the animals' fear. Eliphaz, Job's friend, described the righteous person whom God rescues from harm as one who "need not fear the beasts of the earth," and "the wild animals will be at peace with you" (Job 5:22, 23).

Food for You

Many today teach and believe that we ought to be vegetarians. Some endorse this for health reasons. There is nothing wrong with being vegetarian if one so chooses. In the New Testament era, some believers would not eat meat bought in marketplaces because it had been offered to idols. However, others adhere to this belief because of their worldviews. Hindus, Buddhists, and New Agers believe in reincarnation, meaning that our lives may come back in the form of animal life. Some actually worship animals, as Hindus worship cows. So they are vegetarians by conviction. Also Seventh-Day Adventists, according to the teachings of prophetess and founder Ellen G. White, think we should go back to the pre-Fall situation of being vegetarians, as they interpret the silence concerning eating meat in Genesis 1:29.

However, God has given us animals for our blessing and good, including our food. Animals were not made in God's image nor do they have eternal souls.[11] They are irrational creatures of instinct that go to destruction (2 Pet. 2:12). Therefore, it is legitimate to use animals for medical research, as beasts of burden, for transportation, and other uses for the benefit of humanity. However, we must take care of our animals and be kind to them (Prov. 12:10; Luke 13:15;

14:5) in exercising dominion over them and establishing order in the world. Animals honor and praise the LORD (Ps. 148:10; Isa. 43:20), and are instruments in his hands for destruction or peace (Hosea 2:12, 18).

After the Flood, God expanded people's dominion over the animals by giving them to humans for food. God said, "Everything that lives and moves will be food for you. Just as I gave you the green plants, I now give you everything" (Gen. 9:3). Some believe Adam and Eve were vegetarians because no explicit mention of eating animals was made (Gen. 1:29). However, Abel likely ate his animal sacrifice, as well as the flocks he raised (Gen. 4:2). Some commentators think that the antediluvian people probably ate meat, even though God had not endorsed it (Gen. 4:20). Others, like Meredith Kline, believe eating animal flesh was permitted from the beginning. This becomes clear in the text's broader context. The assignment of plants for food in Genesis 1:29 was not restrictive to only that. The passage has a theme of humankind's kingship over the animal and plant realms. Fish, birds, and every other living creature (Gen. 1:28) submit to people's rule in various ways, including providing for their food. God described the distinctive contribution of plants in that they feed both animals and people. Thus, humans are lords over that realm. There is also a literary purpose in mentioning permission to eat every seed-bearing plant and fruit. It prepares the reader for the prohibition against eating of the fruit of the tree of knowledge of good and evil (Gen. 2:16, 17).

God saying in Genesis 9:3, "I now give you everything," was a new mandate to eat even unclean animals in the common-grace world. No reason was given as to why people were now allowed to eat all the animals. But it appeared to be due to some change in the human situation after the Flood. Some food was prohibited by the ceremonial law, but in the age of the gospel, it was not so (Mark 7:19; Acts 10:9–16). We saw that Noah took seven pairs of ceremonially clean animals into the ark. These were distinguished for the purposes of sacrifices for worship and for food. Under Mosaic Law, commandments were given prohibiting the eating of unclean meat. Those offering animal sacrifices were to eat the meat of the sacrifices. This distinction under the theocracy of Israel was also applied during the theocracy of God over the covenant community in the ark. They were set apart for God. When Noah and his family came out of the ark, God gave them a common-grace covenant to live by until the establishment of the theocracy under Mosaic Law, and all meat eating was permissible. This is again the rule in God's new covenant kingdom of our own day.

Eating meat was endorsed by the practice of Jesus. He fed the five thousand with fish, and he grilled fish over a fire for his disciples after his resurrection (John 21:9). He certainly ate the Paschal lamb at the Passover meal (Mark 14:12). We see through the rest of redemptive history that eating meat was not only endorsed, commanded, and practiced, but also prohibiting meat eating was considered demonic teaching.

Paul instructed Timothy that in latter times demonic teaching will be followed by some who "order them to abstain from certain foods, which God created to be received with thanksgiving by those who believe and who know the truth. For everything God created is good, and nothing is to be rejected if it is received with thanksgiving, because it is consecrated by the word of God and prayer" (1 Tim. 4:3–5).

Now if some believers object to eating meat, we must not judge them. Those with weak faith must do as their own consciences dictate. For instance, if a Christian brother is a convert from Hinduism and never ate meat, we must not put him down for refusing to eat it, something he grew up believing to be repulsive. Or if a sister became a believer out of Islam or Judaism and refuses to eat a delicious slice of ham at a church dinner, we must respect that, for God accepts her. As Paul said,

> "Therefore let us stop passing judgment on one another. Instead,
> make up your mind not to put any stumbling block or obstacle

in your brother's way. As one who is in the Lord Jesus, I am fully
convinced that no food is unclean in itself. But if anyone regards
something as unclean, then for him it is unclean. . . . For the
kingdom of God is not a matter of eating and drinking, but of
righteousness, peace and joy in the Holy Spirit . . . All food is
clean, but it is wrong for a man to eat anything that causes someone else to stumble. It is better not to eat meat or drink wine or
to do anything else that will cause your brother to fall." (Rom.
14:13, 14, 17, 20, 21)

From these instructions, we learn that we must not be judg-
mental toward those who believe differently than we do on matters
of food, and we must not offend one another. These subjects are not
concerned with the essentials of the gospel and so are not important. Since they are morally indifferent issues, we must not allow
them to cause division in the church's fellowship.

No Meat with Lifeblood

The LORD went on to tell Noah, "But you must not eat meat that
has its lifeblood still in it" (Gen. 9:4). This prohibition included not
eating animals that were strangled or died from natural causes (Deut.
14:21). This practice was carried over from Judaism into Islam. A
Muslim *halal* or permissible meat is an animal that has had its throat
cut as it faces Mecca, and the butcher says, "In the name of Allah."

An Egyptian Muslim physician doing research in Philadelphia,
out of concern for eating properly slaughtered meat, asked me if
the slaughterhouses in America electrically shocked cattle or slit
their throats.

A missionary in North Africa was on a bus trip when a passen-
ger's goat was about to die and was gasping for breath. Rather than
lose the animal and not be able to use it, the owner had the bus stop
and wait while he butchered it by the side of the road.

The Old Testament rationale for not eating meat with its blood was that blood had sanctity as a symbol for a life given in a sacrifice. The lives of God's creatures are his, for only he gives them life. Mosaic Law required "that nearly everything be cleansed with blood," for it is only through the shedding of blood that we have forgiveness of sins (Heb. 9:22). Unfortunately, it is this essential concept of substitutionary atonement that has been lost in Islam.

> The Law given to Moses explains the prohibition further.
>
> " 'Any Israelite or any alien living among them who eats any blood—I will set my face against that person who eats blood and will cut him off from his people. For the life of a creature is in the blood, and I have given it to you to make atonement for yourselves on the altar; it is the blood that makes atonement for one's life. Therefore I say to the Israelites, "None of you may eat blood, nor may an alien living among you eat blood." (Lev. 17:10–12)

Blood shed in sacrifices was prohibited from being eaten because of its symbolic role in altar sacrifice. The life value of the animal's blood was in its ransom equivalent for human life. It was used to make atonement for sin, which justly deserved the wrath of God.[12] Thus, eating it was strictly forbidden (Lev. 3:17). The blood atonement on an altar represented one life substituted for another. It was a ritual that pointed forward to the blood sacrifice of the Lamb of God, Jesus Christ, who died on the cross for our sins. Since life in the blood belongs to God, the blood sacrifices could be seen as his gift to sinners, not theirs to him.[13]

Some have seen the prohibition against ingesting blood as suggesting the sacredness of life. This is not a biblical concept, but as Meredith Kline calls it, "some sort of animistic mysticism."[14]

We are privileged today in the age of the gospel to not have to offer animal sacrifices whose blood was smeared on the altar and sprinkled on the ceremonially unclean to sanctify them. Christ has entered the Most Holy Place of the heavenly temple, the very presence of God, with his own shed blood. There he obtained our eternal redemption, if we have trusted in him. Having done so, we now are cleansed through the blood of Christ, who through the eternal Spirit offered himself unblemished to God. Through his mediation, he cleanses "our consciences from acts that lead to death, so that we may serve the living God!" (Heb. 9:14).

Matthew Henry interprets eating meat with its lifeblood as meaning that we are not to eat raw flesh. But this seems to be a misunderstanding. It probably means that the blood of an animal must be drained out before butchering and eating it (Lev. 17:13). We see an example of this when the Israelite soldiers were exhausted after striking down the Philistines under Saul's leadership.

> They pounced on the plunder and, taking sheep, cattle and calves, they butchered them on the ground and ate them, together with the blood. Then someone said to Saul, "Look, the men are sinning against the LORD by eating meat that has blood in it."
>
> "You have broken faith," he said. "Roll a large stone over here at once." Then he said, "Go out among the men and tell them, 'Each of you bring me your cattle and sheep, and slaughter them here and eat them. Do not sin against the LORD by eating meat with blood still in it.' "
>
> So everyone brought his ox that night and slaughtered it there. (1 Sam. 14:32–34)

The large stone was rolled over for the purpose of having the slain animal elevated so that the blood could drain out. Thus, they would keep from sinning against the LORD's command.

In the New Testament, after the gospel had come to the Gentiles, a church council (general assembly) met in Jerusalem to decide what was required of Gentiles in joining the church. Were

Gentiles required to be circumcised and keep the Law of Moses? The council sent a letter to Gentile believers saying, "You are to abstain from food sacrificed to idols, *from blood, from the meat of strangled animals* and from sexual immorality" (Acts 15:29, emphasis added). At the council, James explained this decision of having moderation by both Jewish and Gentile believers by saying, "For Moses has been preached in every city from the earliest times and is read in the synagogues on every Sabbath" (Acts 15:21). In other words, throughout the Roman Empire, Jewish communities had preached the Law of Moses. The Gentiles were aware of what the Jews believed. As Gentile believers, they ought not to offend the scruples of the Jewish Christian community by eating meat offered to idols, blood, and strangled animals, whose blood had not been drained. Yet Gentiles should not be bound by Jewish ceremonial law, such as circumcision. Not eating blood was part of the Jewish ceremonial law, which had been fulfilled in Christ through his sacrifice for our sins. However, at the time of the Jerusalem council, the Temple altar worship was still in effect. The Noahic covenantal legislation anticipated the ceremonial law, already seen as well in the blood sacrifices offered by Abel and Seth (Gen. 4:4, 26). The prohibition of Genesis 9:4 was only for those within the orbit of the earthly altar of sacrifice, thereby honoring it. Thus, it was not for everyone in the world but only for those in the covenant community. As long as an earthly altar of sacrifice remained, the prohibition against eating blood remained.

Christ abolished the first law in order to establish the second, the sacrifice of himself once for all (Heb. 10:9, 10). The period between Christ's ascension and the end of the sacrificial system in the Temple with its destruction in judgment in AD 70 was a transitional period. Acts 10 and 15 represent turning points in the covenant community from living in a theocratic organization of life into the common-grace world all Christians live in today. With a vision from heaven, Peter was instructed that association and table fellowship with Gentiles was not prohibited anymore (Acts 10, especially v. 28). Thus, the clean/unclean distinction was abolished in the culture at large but maintained in regard to worship at the Lord's Table (1 Cor. 10:14–21; 11:25–29) and acceptance into Christian fellowship (2 Cor. 6:14–16; 2 John 10, 11).

Today we are free to eat blood sausage. But I would not eat it in front of my Jewish, Muslim, Hindu, or Buddhist friends, so as not to be offensive to their sensibilities and thus sin against Christ (Rom. 14:13–21; 1 Cor. 8; 10:23, 24, 31–33). Early New Testament testimony was that the restriction against eating blood was soon repealed (Rom. 14:14; 1 Cor. 10:25–31) or never taught among Gentiles who were outside the orbit of Temple worship. Its temporary New Testament application appears to have been for those within the sphere of Temple altar sacrifice from Jerusalem to Antioch.

After the Flood of judgment against sin, which resulted in the death of all except those on the ark, God gave a covenant of preservation of life. The stipulation of the covenant dealt with the continuation of life—that the earth might be filled with the image of God, that people would be protected by the fear of humans in the animals, that blood was prohibited from being eaten because of its role in altar sacrifice, and the sustenance of life by animals becoming humanity's food.

In being part of a life-affirming covenant, we see an image in the lifeblood of animals of how we obtain eternal life. The spilled blood of an animal as a sacrificial offering symbolized the atonement for our sins we have in Jesus Christ. He gave his life for us, just as the blood of animals was given but life blood was only a symbolic substitute for sin. Knowing this, we should constantly be reminded of our salvation every time we eat meat. By faith we must believe that all of life, even eternal life, comes from God through Christ.

SCRIPTURE READING:

PSALM 8

Discussion Questions

1. How does the common-grace covenant of being fruitful and filling the earth emphasize the importance of the family in society? How has that basic institution been eroded in today's society?

2. What is God's purpose in the mandate to fill the earth? How ought Christians to respond to this today? Why is it important?

3. How may we appropriately use, care for, and protect animals in our dominion over them?

4. Is it appropriate for Christians to eat meat? How about eating animal blood? What brought about a change in this legislation for Christians?

5. Are there times when we ought to restrain our freedom in what we eat for the sake of others?

6. What symbolism may we find in the blood of animals?

7. Why are animal sacrifices no longer necessary for our worship?

Notes

1. Derek Kidner, *Genesis*, vol. 1 of *The Tyndale Old Testament Commentaries* (Downers Grove, Ill.: InterVarsity, 1967), 100.

2. Henry R. Van Til, *The Calvinistic Concept of Culture* (Grand Rapids: Baker, 1972), 30, 31.

3. Robert L. Sassone, *Handbook on Population*, 3rd ed. (n.p., 1973), 184.

4. Patrick Johnstone and Jason Mandryk, *Operation World*, 21st century ed. (Waynesboro, Ga.: Paternoster, 2001), 1.

5. Ken Dilanian, "Italy Is Baffled by Birth Drop-off," *Philadelphia Inquirer*, December 23, 2002, A8, B.

6. Genaro C. Armas, "Record Number of Women Childless," *Philadelphia Inquirer,* October 25, 2003, A1.

7. Sassone, *Handbook on Population,* 100.

8. As of the 2000 census, India's population density is 819/sq. mi. (320/sq. km.) while New Jersey's is 1,134/sq. mi. New Jersey is the most densely populated American state.

9. Jodi Enda, "Lawmakers to Fight for Aid to Population Agency," *The Philadelphia Inquirer,* 23 July 2002, A12, C.

10. An exception to this has been in Romania, where women were forced to have large families under the rule of communist dictator Nicolae Ceausescu. However, currently the country is in population decline and a declining economy.

11. However, it does appear from Scripture that animals will be in the future consummation of the Messianic kingdom (Isa. 11:6–9; 65:25). But will we be feasting on them then as well, as heaven is depicted as a grand feast?

12. Meredith G. Kline, *Kingdom Prologue* (Overland Park, Kans.: Two Age Press, 2000), 256.

13. Kidner, *Genesis,* 101.

14. Kline, *Kingdom Prologue,* 256.

Accountability to God for Life

Genesis 9:5–7

5 *"And for your lifeblood I will surely demand an accounting. I will demand an accounting from every animal. And from each man, too, I will demand an accounting for the life of his fellow man.*

6 *"Whoever sheds the blood of man,*
by man shall his blood be shed;
for in the image of God
has God made man.

7 *"As for you, be fruitful and increase in number; multiply on the earth and increase upon it."*

SINCE ADAM AND EVE'S fall in the Garden of Eden, humanity's hearts are bent on evil. It manifested itself in a profound way when Cain murdered his brother Abel (Gen. 4:8) and disregarded any responsibility. A few generations later, Lamech boasted about killing a young man (Gen. 4:23). Wickedness continued to increase on the earth. Finally, the LORD brought judgment on the great violence prevalent in the days of Noah prior to the Flood (Gen. 6:11, 13). After Noah and his sons and their wives were delivered from the Flood by the ark, God sought to stem the spread of violence by holding every person and animal accountable for the lifeblood of others. In doing that, he gave people the responsibility of exercising judgment on the guilty. In this way, men and women were to share in God's rule over his creatures. God blessed them so they could multiply and fill the earth.

⁓ Accounting for Human Lifeblood

God limited the rights of people over his creatures, including other men and women, because their lives were his alone. The reason given for why one who murders should be put to death is because "for in the image of God has God made man" (Gen. 9:6). We are made in the image of God. This image was not totally destroyed after the Fall. Yes, it was distorted from its original perfection of righteousness and holiness, but it is still there. Being made in God's image means that we have eternal souls, a sense of morality, ability to communicate with God and others, and intelligence and creativity that is unique to us as opposed to the animals. We were created to be God's representatives on earth as his image bearers and the focal point of his kingdom. Therefore we are very precious to God. Every person is worthy of honor, respect, and dignity. Taking the life of a murderer emphasizes the sanctity of human life, and it preserves the race for future multiplication.

Because these things are true, God holds us accountable for the lifeblood of others. Blood is symbolic of life, for it carries all the necessities of life to every cell of the body. For this reason, as we saw in Genesis 9:4, people were not to eat meat with its lifeblood still in it. Spilled blood points to the sacrificial life given for our sins in the death of the Messiah on the cross.

Since we are made in God's image, he will demand an accounting for our lifeblood from ourselves, from animals, and from others. The threefold usage of *demand* or *require* illustrates the compensation God requires from the murderer, which is nothing less than his life. God himself is the defender of human life. When Cain murdered Abel, Cain denied responsibility for his brother. "The LORD said, "What have you done? Listen! Your brother's blood cries out to me from the ground. Now you are under a curse and driven from the ground, which opened its mouth to receive your brother's blood from your hand' " (Gen. 4:10, 11). Clearly, we are responsible for our fellow men.

First, God will demand an accounting from us for our own lives. "And for your lifeblood I will surely demand an accounting" (Gen. 9:5). We may not take our own lives. We are accountable to God for hastening our own deaths. We do not have that right because God gave us our lives. Only he has the right to take our lives in his own timing.

Sometimes people go into deep depression or are mentally disturbed, even among those who profess faith in Christ. If a Christian commits suicide, does that mean he has committed an unforgivable sin and will go to hell? This is Roman Catholic and Islamic teaching. I think not. Certainly, suicide is an awful sin and dishonor before our Creator. But all Christians who die also have sins they may not have confessed or even realized they had committed. Yet through our faith in Christ, even if our faith is as small as a mustard seed, we can have confidence before God that our sins have been forgiven. Christ ever intercedes for us before the Father (Rom. 8:34).

Recently, four Chinese dowsed themselves with gasoline in Tiananmen Square and set themselves on fire to call attention to the issue of freedom for practicing Falun Gong in China. Killing oneself like this is a demonically influenced act. It is destroying a life given by God meant for glorifying him through good works. Some societies offer little hope to people in despair, and the vast majority of its people have no knowledge of the God who made them. Therefore, in a country like China, we have 40 percent of the world's suicides.

Second, God will demand an accounting for human lifeblood from every animal. God said, "I will demand an accounting from every animal" (Gen. 9:5). To show the great care God has for the lives of persons, even animals must die for killing them. The Mosaic Law states, "If a bull gores a man or a woman to death, the bull must be stoned to death, and its meat must not be eaten" (Exod. 21:28). A recent example of seeing this principle put into practice was when a child squeezed into a tiger's zoo cage and was killed by the tiger. The security guard shot the tiger to death. Even though we may want to protect rare animals, we also have responsibility to hold them accountable for human lives.

Third, we are accountable to God for the lifeblood of others. God will exact justice from the one who murders. This responsibility for carrying out justice has been given to human government.

America today is one of the most violent countries in the world, after Colombia, South Africa, and Brazil. "In the last quarter of a century, almost 500,000 murders have been committed in the United States."[1] But most of the violence in our country is not what we read about in the newspapers or hear on the evening news. In Proverbs we see that among the things most hateful to the LORD are "hands that shed innocent blood" (Prov. 6:17). Surely, the innocents whose blood has been shed are the one and a half million babies aborted each year. This is detestable to God, and our country will be held accountable for this grievous evil. People are accountable at many different levels, from the mother and father of the child, to the abortionists, to lawmakers, to judges, to churches that refuse to speak out against this evil.

Proverbs admonishes us saying,

"Speak up for those who cannot speak for themselves,
    for the rights of all who are destitute.
Speak up and judge fairly;
    defend the rights of the poor and needy." (Prov. 31:8, 9)

Are not the unborn among those who cannot speak for themselves?

As David described the wonders of God's knowledge, power, presence, and works, he praised God for the wonder of how we are made.

For you created my inmost being;
    you knit me together in my mother's womb.
I praise you because I am fearfully and wonderfully made;
    your works are wonderful,
    I know that full well.
My frame was not hidden from you
    when I was made in the secret place.
When I was woven together in the depths of the earth,
    your eyes saw my unformed body.
All the days ordained for me
    were written in your book
    before one of them came to be. (Ps. 139:13–16)

We see described here the wonders of God's hand in creating each person in his image. What he has created is wonderful. It is not something we have the option to destroy. He sees the unformed body of the developing embryo in the womb. This is not just a piece of disposable tissue, but a separate individual given a soul with the capacity to have a relationship with God. By ten weeks after conception, all the fingers and toes are formed, with fingerprints, too. All the days of our lives, even of every unborn child, has been known to God before we were even conceived. He has a purpose for our lives.

But today it is common for babies to be aborted or killed in infanticide simply because they are of the wrong sex. This is especially true in China because of the one-child policy and in India because of their strong preference for male children for cultural and economic reasons. "It is estimated that up to five million baby girls are aborted every year in India. . . . The sex-determination tests were banned in the country in 1994, but they continue to be performed and are blamed for a dramatic drop in the male–female birth ratio."[2] China currently has ten million abortions per year, 97 percent of them girls. The one child policy has had the result that "in 2000 there were 90 million marriageable unmarried men; in some areas young men outnumber young women by 30–40%."[3] "There are now 120 million more boys under the age of 15 than girls."[4] This is resulting in many social problems.

The mother of celebrity singer Celine Dion had considered aborting her since this was her fourteenth child. But after consulting her priest, she kept the baby, whom she dearly loved. Of course, Celine Dion has now become a household name around the world for her beautiful singing. Examples like this can be multiplied many times over. Each life can be a blessing.

Much has been said in recent years concerning the "mercy killings" of Jack Kevorkian. Mercy killing is not something anyone has the right to do. Suffering is part of life, a lot God has given to some to endure. We must wait on God's timing for our deaths. Now I don't believe this means that when a person is only able to survive on a life-support system, such as a respirator, is brain dead, and has no hope of recovery, that there won't be a time to ultimately pull the plug. Thus, a person is allowed to die a natural death, and his family is saved from prolonged grief, extreme hardship, and financial ruin. But what is happening in today's society is that the old and sick who seem to have lost their usefulness are being allowed to die in degrading ways such as starvation, withholding food from them, or giving them lethal doses of drugs. Since 2002, euthanasia has been legalized in Holland, the first country to do so. It also is commonly practiced in other European countries. Where is the humanity and dignity in that? Euthanasia is murder.

Recently, a man delivering pizza was shot and killed as he was robbed of thirty-five dollars. The victim was the father of three young children and was working three jobs to support his family. Such a murderer demonstrates not only contempt for the person he kills but also hatred for God who made him in his image. He has made greed the god he worships.

∼ Capital Punishment

God holds us accountable for our sins, particularly for murder. During the theocracy of the nation of Israel, God demanded the execution of those who committed premeditated murder (Exod. 21:12–14; Num. 35:16–21, 30, 31).

The prophet Zechariah, son of Jehoiada the priest, was stoned to death by order of King Joash after saying that since the people of Judah had forsaken the LORD, he would forsake them. As Zechariah lay dying, he said, "May the LORD see this and call you to account" (2 Chron. 24:22). Consequently, the LORD allowed the Aramean army to invade Judah, and judgment was executed on Joash. He was severely wounded, then his officials conspired against him for killing Zechariah and killed him in his bed (2 Chron. 24:24, 25).

As the LORD promised, he sent the invading armies of Babylonia, Aramea, Moab, and Ammon against Judah for the sins of King Manasseh. He "shed so much innocent blood that he filled Jerusalem from end to end" (2 Kings 21:16). Shedding innocent blood was a sin God would not pardon in Manasseh (2 Kings 24:3, 4). Therefore, a king, president, or governor should not pardon one of his citizens who has committed murder, unless there are extenuating circumstances or some doubt as to guilt.

Genesis 9:6 is a foundational verse in support of the idea of capital punishment for murder. It is not simply stating a fact. Human responsibility is found in the parallelism of the verse's structure and in the instrument called for to carry out justice.

a   *"Whoever sheds*
  b   *the blood*
    c   *of man,*
    c' *by man*
  b' *shall his blood*
a' *be shed."*

This structure suggests the law of an eye for an eye, a tooth for a tooth. The human community is specifically designated as the one through whom the murderer's blood was to be shed. Thus, God's demand for accounting from a murderer is that justice be executed through the community agency as his minister.[5]

The context of this passage makes it clear that this mandate was not temporary but enduring. It was given in the context of the Noahic covenant, in which seasons were instituted as part of the natural order (Gen. 8:22); the fear of humans by animals has continued as their basic relationship (Gen. 9:2); the eating of meat is still permitted (Gen. 9:3); the violation of the image of God in persons continues as the reason for the death penalty (Gen. 9:6); and no flood has again destroyed the earth, with the rainbow as a pledge (Gen. 9:16, 17). At some later point, God does not deal with a murderer with immediate divine punishment but has continued to give people responsibility to carry out justice. Simply because the Law of Moses incorporated capital punishment and this ceremonial and civil law has been abolished does not mean that the law given prior to Moses has been done away with. Noah was the head of a whole new generation of humanity. His covenant mandate was for all his posterity and has continued to be carried out by peoples all over the

world who never received the Law of Moses. This shows the enduring nature of this mandate.[6]

Although some temporary limited aspects were in the Noahic
covenant in regard to eating blood, this does not mean that every
element of the covenant was temporary. The circumcision rite in the
Abrahamic covenant and the sacrificial system in the Mosaic
covenant are now fulfilled, yet they continue to play major roles in
our understanding of our redemption. Also, the power granted by
God to human authorities to bear the sword gives evidence of the
abiding importance of the sanctity of life.

Despite the continuance of the Noahic legislation to our day,
the mandate has not been widely practiced in the United States. Of
the half a million murders in the past quarter century, "slightly
more than 7,000 of the murderers received death sentences and
fewer than 800 have been executed."[7] When punishment for the
guilty is taken lightly, the people lose all fear of recrimination for
their crimes. Also, by lightly punishing the guilty, where can the victim's family find justice for their loss?

When Jesus was arrested in the Garden of Gethsemane, one of
his companions took out his sword and cut off the ear of the high
priest's servant. " 'Put your sword back in its place,' Jesus said to
him, 'for all who draw the sword will die by the sword' " (Matt.
26:52). Jesus here confirmed the mandate given to Noah, that murderers will be held accountable by the sword of the governing
authorities (cf. Paul's teaching, Rom. 13:4).

There may also be the implication that violence begets violence.
Laurent Kabila, the president of the Democratic Republic of the
Congo, the former Zaire, was murdered in his palace by one of his
own bodyguards. We can understand how this may be the consequences of a bloody coup d'etat that brought him to power and the
oppression and continual civil war that kept him there the following four years. Although the violent often seem to get away with it,
ultimately they will receive their just due.

In carrying out capital punishment, we must be careful not to put to death someone who is innocent. As the Mosaic Law stated, "Have nothing to do with a false charge and do not put an innocent or honest person to death, for I will not acquit the guilty" (Exod. 23:7). Sometimes our fear of capital punishment has to do with fear of putting innocent persons to death. However, we have more to fear from guilty people being wrongly freed than from the small number who are wrongfully imprisoned and the miniscule number who are actually executed. Today we have DNA tests that can often be used to establish innocence. The Law of Moses also required that there be witnesses before allowing the execution of a murderer. The testimony of only one witness was not enough (Num. 35:30). Therefore, if we have any doubt as to a person's guilt, we ought not to have him or her put to death.

Family members should not be punished for the guilt of another member of the family, as was often practiced in the ancient world. Even today family feuds in certain areas of the world have led to decades of murders being committed between opposing clans. The Law of Moses said, "Fathers shall not be put to death for their children, nor children put to death for their fathers; each is to die for his own sin" (Deut. 24:16). Capital punishment for apostatizing from one's faith or blaspheming its prophet or holy book (as in Islam) is totally contrary to the freedom of conscience and belief that ought to be a basic human right given by God to all. Only God can ultimately convince someone of his truth. Also, sexual sins of adultery, rape, and sodomy are no longer capital offenses, as under Mosaic Law (cf. John 8:1–11), although they are extremely offensive to God's holiness.

∾ Murder and Eternal Life

Jesus gave us a deeper understanding of what it means to keep the commandment not to murder in his Sermon on the Mount.

"You have heard that it was said to the people long ago, 'Do not murder, and anyone who murders will be subject to judgment.' But I tell you that anyone who is angry with his brother will be subject to judgment. Again, anyone who says to his brother, 'Raca,' is answerable to the Sanhedrin. But anyone who says, 'You fool!' will be in danger of the fire of hell." (Matt. 5:21–22)

Raca was an Aramaic term of contempt. Jesus said that by even becoming angry and cursing someone made in God's image, we are breaking God's commandment not to murder. We are murdering that person in our hearts. God sees our hearts and judges our intentions. Therefore, even if we have not literally murdered someone, we have done so in our hearts and are guilty before God. John confirmed this when he said, "Anyone who hates his brother is a murderer, and you know that no murderer has eternal life in him" (1 John 3:15).

We must all repent and seek God's mercy through the blood atonement of Jesus Christ for our sins, which he suffered on the cross. In God's set purpose, he allowed Jesus to be murdered for us (Acts 2:23). God took our sins so seriously, including murder, that he sent his Son to be put to death in our places. For God's justice to be satisfied, only God's sinless Son could bear his wrath against sin and yet come out victoriously through his resurrection. For Jesus' death to be applied to our own sins, we must humbly come to him in repentance and faith. Then "the blood of Jesus . . . purifies us from all sin. . . . If we confess our sins, he is faithful and just and will forgive us our sins and purify us from all unrighteousness" (1 John 1:7, 9).

⁓ Judicial Authority

What was new about God's mandate to Noah regarding putting a murderer to death was his sharing his rule over people with people. Up until then God had reserved all judgment for himself. He had punished humanity with the judgment of the Flood. Now he shared his power with men and women, granting them power over life and death if a person or animal was guilty of murder. By God endowing people with judicial authority, rulers are standing as God's representatives. Formerly, on their creation, men and women were made in God's image and given the cultural mandate to have dominion over all the earth. Now they were not only administrators but also were given judicial authority. This was the first establishment of human government. It was the foundation for government by the state. When we serve in the military, on the police force, in public office, on the judiciary, or on a jury, we participate in human government established by God that has authority over humanity. As shown before, subsequent legislation given to Israel affirmed the responsibilities of human authority to execute capital punishment on the murderer (Exod. 21:12; Num. 35:16–21).

The governing authorities are instituted by God to carry out justice in this life. They have the mandate to legislate and uphold morality. Human authority is dependent on God for its existence. Paul wrote about this saying, "Everyone must submit himself to the governing authorities, for there is no authority except that which God has established. The authorities that exist have been established by God. . . . But if you do wrong, be afraid, for he does not bear the sword for nothing. He is God's servant, an agent of wrath to bring punishment on the wrongdoer" (Rom. 13:1, 4). Obviously, the governing authorities bear the sword to bring judgment, including capital punishment. This could be extended to indicate the authority of a government to maintain order on both national and international levels. On occasion governments need to exercise force to keep the peace and restrain evil, thus the need for an army.

Peter also instructed believers to submit to authority.

> Submit yourselves for the Lord's sake to every authority instituted
> among men: whether to the king, as the supreme authority, or to

governors, who are sent by him to punish those who do wrong and to commend those who do right. . . . Show proper respect to everyone: Love the brotherhood of believers, fear God, honor the king. (1 Pet. 2:13, 14, 17)

Here again we see that governing authorities are established by God "to punish those who do wrong." We submit to the authorities "for the Lord's sake." In doing so, we acknowledge our fear and honor of God. In disobeying human authority, such as the government, we are indirectly disobeying God, who has established that authority for our good. The state was instituted by God to restrain the evil found in every person.

~ Blessing to Multiply

The conclusion to the middle section of the common-grace Noahic covenant emphasized again the importance of filling the earth. The purposes of God given first to Adam and Eve and then to Noah and his sons were to "be fruitful and increase in number; multiply on the earth and increase upon it" (Gen. 9:7). God concluded his mandate to Noah by repeating the blessing he began with. God's purposes are for human life to flourish and multiply, filling the earth for whom he made it. People committing suicide, abortion, infanticide, euthanasia, and murder continually contravene this.

May we be faithful in fulfilling God's mandate to honor him by upholding human dignity in all situations. Since we are made in God's image, we must demand an accounting for each life as God does, for he has given us that authority through human government. As God's image bearers, we work our status out in cultural life by having civic roles in human society.

As for those of us who are now accountable to God for our own sin of destroying his image in people, may he show us his mercy as we fall at his feet in repentance and faith. The LORD said to the people of Judah and Jerusalem, which had become full of murderers (Isa. 1:21):

"Your hands are full of blood;
  wash and make yourselves clean. . . .
"Come now, let us reason together,"
  says the LORD.
"Though your sins are like scarlet,
  they shall be as white as snow;
though they are red as crimson,
  they shall be like wool." (Isa. 1:15, 16, 18)

What a precious promise and hope from God that we can all cling to as we come under conviction of our own sins. Lord, have mercy on us!

SCRIPTURE READING:
ISAIAH 59

Discussion Questions

1. Why does God take the sin of murder so seriously?
2. Is capital punishment a legitimate form of restraint and punishment for evil?
3. Is the Noahic covenantal legislation still in effect today?
4. Did we have a part in the murder of Jesus?
5. What authority has God given to men and women that we share with him? How are we to exercise that authority?
6. Having come under conviction for participating in some form of murder ourselves, what recourse do we have?

Notes

1. Joshua Marquis, " 'Innocents Executed,' a Myth That Deserves Death Penalty," *Philadelphia Inquirer,* January 3, 2002, B, A23.

2. Dominic Aquila, ed., *PCA News, Information and Resources* (PCANEWS.com Newsletter), August 20, 2002.

3. Patrick Johnstone and Jason Mandryk, *Operation World*, 21st century ed. (Waynesboro, Ga.: Paternoster, 2001), 162.

4. James Kraus, ed., *The Church Around the World* 33, no. 7 (June 2003).

5. O. Palmer Robertson, *The Christ of the Covenants* (Phillipsburg, N.J.: Presbyterian and Reformed, 1980), 118.

6. William H. Baker, *Worthy of Death* (Chicago: Moody, 1973), 39, 40, 133–135.

7. Marquis, "Innocents Executed," A23.

A Rainbow of Remembrance

Genesis 9:8–17

8 *Then God said to Noah and to his sons with him:* **9** *"I now establish my covenant with you and with your descendants after you* **10** *and with every living creature that was with you—the birds, the livestock and all the wild animals, all those that came out of the ark with you—every living creature on earth.* **11** *I establish my covenant with you: Never again will all life be cut off by the waters of a flood; never again will there be a flood to destroy the earth."*

   12 *And God said, "This is the sign of the covenant I am making between me and you and every living creature with you, a covenant for all generations to come:* **13** *I have set my rainbow in the clouds, and it will be the sign of the covenant between me and the earth.* **14** *Whenever I bring clouds over the earth and the rainbow appears in the clouds,* **15** *I will remember my covenant between me and you and all living creatures* *of every kind. Never again will the waters become a flood to destroy all life.* **16** *Whenever the rainbow appears in the clouds, I will see it and remember the everlasting covenant between God and all living creatures of every kind on the earth."*

    17 *So God said to Noah, "This is the sign of the covenant I have established between me and all life on the earth."*

WHEN A NON-CHRISTIAN sees a rainbow, he usually responds with, "Oh, isn't that beautiful!" But his thoughts rarely go deeper than that. We frequently see that children have rainbows in their coloring books. It gives them an opportunity to use many colors to complete their pictures. A political group has included the name "Rainbow" in its name to reflect the diversity they seek to embrace. Others have taken a rainbow as a symbol for including deviant sexual behavior to be accepted as normal and socially acceptable. But all of these views of rainbows miss the important revelation of God's message to us that it conveys. Clearly, rainbows are a part of God's general revelation of himself.

> The heavens declare the glory of God;
>   the skies proclaim the work of his hands. (Ps. 19:1)

But it is only through God's special revelation in the Scriptures that we can understand the significance attached to it. There we find it is a sign of God's common-grace covenant love. By means of a rainbow, God promises to remember to never destroy the earth with a flood again.

∿ A Covenant

To confirm to Noah and his sons after the devastation and holocaust of the Flood that there would be a prosperous continuance of the human race, God made a covenant with them, with their descendants, and with all the animals. This covenant was confirmed with a visible sign. This sign will be seen throughout the ages as a reminder to God of his promise to never destroy the earth again by flood. As an everlasting covenant, it will last even to the end of the world.

Three major types of covenants are found in the Bible. These are royal grant, which is unconditional; parity, between equals; and suzerain-vassal, which is conditional as between a great king and one of his subject kings. God's covenant with Noah, his descendants, and every living thing was an unconditional royal grant. It was a promise from God given to us by his grace, which was not earned or deserved. Since it was given to all creation equally, whether people are righteous and in the faith or not, we call it a manifestation of God's common grace. Similarly, God "causes his sun to rise on the evil and the good, and sends rain on the righteous and the unrighteous" (Matt. 5:45). God's special saving grace is illustrated with Noah when God made a covenant with him just prior to entering the ark (Gen. 6:18), and the ark became a type of God's kingdom being saved through judgment.

God used signs to confirm his covenants with humanity. The first covenantal sign made with Noah was in his entering the ark with the pairs of animals and passing through the judgment of the Flood (Gen. 6:18). A sign of the covenant made with Abraham was initially made with the firepot going between split animals (Gen. 15:17, 18) and then by circumcision (Gen. 17:1–14). A sign of the covenant made on Mount Sinai between God and his people Israel was that they keep the Sabbath holy as a day in which they did no work, indicating that the LORD sanctifies his people (Exod. 31:13, 17). The signs of the new covenant are baptism with water (Col. 2:11, 12) and the Lord's Supper (Matt. 26:27, 28; 1 Cor. 11:25). Some signs were already in existence before they became symbolic of the covenant, such as the Sabbath, circumcision, baptism, and possibly the rainbow. But with the confirming of the covenants, they were given new significance. They were signs confirming God's faithfulness.

The fact that God himself will be reminded of his covenant promise by the appearance of the rainbow illustrates that his covenant signs "are real vehicles of his grace, that they have power and essential worth not only with men, but also *before God*."[1] This being so, it confirms the view that the sacraments of baptism and the Lord's Supper are means of grace as well, as the Holy Spirit applies their benefits to us through our faith. God is reminded of his covenant promises to us so when we participate in the sacraments, he sees the symbolism of the blood of Christ applied to the washing away of our sins. As Jesus intercedes for us as our High Priest, God the Father sees Jesus' wounds pleading for us that our sins are forgiven. These covenantal signs give us assurance that God will do what he has promised. The absolute sureness of God's covenant promises is compared in Jeremiah to his covenant with day and night and the fixed laws of heaven and earth (Jer. 33:25). They will undoubtedly continue to the end of time. David, too, praised God, singing, "The LORD is faithful to all his promises and loving toward all he has made" (Ps. 145:13).

Significantly, God always initiated making a covenant with humankind. Through the covenants, God's condescending favor is magnified, and he further reveals himself to us. We come to appreciate that although God is high and mighty, he condescends to deal with puny people. We, in turn, see our obedience as a reasonable service we owe the Lord. God made a covenant not only with Noah and his sons but also with all their descendants. Not only was it made with those who responded in faith but also with "every living creature." This is an indication that God can take into his covenant even those who are not yet conscious of their covenantal relationship or have the ability to give their consent, such as infants. Such a relationship is seen in both the circumcision and baptism of infants.

ᔎ A Covenant of Mercy and Comfort

The covenant God made with Noah and his family demonstrated his mercy on the human race rather than bringing judgment on them. After smelling the aroma of the altar sacrifices, God was pleased and promised to never again curse the ground or destroy every living thing (Gen. 8:21). In the immediate past, God brought down his wrath on sin in the judgment of the Flood. Now with the establishment of his covenant of common grace to not destroy the earth again by a flood, God entrusted the judgment of taking human life to human government. This was asserted when God said, "Whoever sheds the blood of man, by man shall his blood be shed" (Gen. 9:6). The violence on the earth particularly grieved the LORD (Gen. 6:11, 13). The earth had become polluted through the spilled blood on it. Through human government, God extended grace to us so we are not all destroyed. Although human wickedness has not diminished since the days of Noah, God's judgment is restrained through his covenant promise. He is keeping back the floodwaters by his word, patiently waiting until the end of the age when he will renew heaven and earth through fire.

God's covenant, as seen in the beautiful rainbow, came as a great comfort to Noah after the trauma of the Flood. All the civilization that he had known was wiped out. He must have had emotional wounds on seeing everything devastated. With God's repetition, "I establish my covenant with you" (Gen. 9:11) and "This is the sign of the covenant I am making between me and you" (v. 12) said several times, God reassured Noah because of his wounded soul. God assured him he would never again destroy the earth by a flood. Although this was a temporal promise, God meant to make us believe that he will provide us a place to live on earth until we are gathered together in the new heaven and earth.

Sometimes we too become so wounded by events that occur in our lives that we despair. But God's covenant rainbow reminds us

that God is still good, and he has good in store for us. He is holding back his judgment for a while longer to show us his mercy. Paul
confirmed this when he pointed out that the riches of God's kindness, tolerance, and patience lead us to repentance (Rom. 2:4). Noah
became the mediator of God's mercy to all creation. In a sense, we
can see Noah as a type of the mediatorship of Jesus for our salvation. He was faithful to the LORD's calling, and it was through him
that God's mercy came to all.

The comfort Noah received from the rainbow is a source of
comfort for us as well. Noah was a source of comfort to his family,
too, as the meaning of his name indicated. Having received comfort
from God through his covenant promise, he could comfort others.
We who are in Christ can do the same. As Paul said, "For just as the
sufferings of Christ flow over into our lives, so also through Christ
our comfort overflows" (2 Cor. 1:5).

The LORD spoke words of hope and encouragement to his
covenant people through Isaiah,

> "To me this is like the days of Noah,
>   when I swore that the waters of Noah would never again cover
>   the earth.
> So now I have sworn not to be angry with you,
>   never to rebuke you again.
> Though the mountains be shaken
>   and the hills be removed,
> yet my unfailing love for you will not be shaken
>   nor my covenant of peace be removed,"
>   says the LORD, who has compassion on you. (Isa. 54:9, 10)

After punishing Israel for her sins, described earlier in Isaiah, God
promised to comfort her and direct his wrath against the nations of
Assyria and Babylon, represented by unbelievers of today. Although
"the mountains be shaken and the hills be removed" at the end of the

age with the earth's final destruction by fire, "yet even then God's loving-kindness shall not depart from Israel, nor the berith [covenant] of his peace be removed."[2]

The same promise is true for us as children of God. Although once we were God's enemies, he has forgiven our sins and has promised to love us forever. Jesus has already borne our sins on himself, taking the anger of God against sin through his death on the cross. So rather than being rebuked and suffering God's judgment, as did those in the Flood, we will be comforted and lovingly welcomed into the throne room of God's kingdom. Then we will have peace with God through Christ, a peace that will not be broken. Nothing can separate us from the love of God. As Paul wrote, "For I am convinced that neither death nor life, neither angels nor demons, neither the present nor the future, nor any powers, neither height nor depth, nor anything else in all creation, will be able to separate us from the love of God that is in Christ Jesus our Lord" (Rom. 8:38, 39).

∼ The Rainbow: A Sign of the Covenant

The sign of the covenant God made with Noah, his descendants (Gen. 9:9, 12), every living creature (vv. 10–12), and the earth (v. 13) was a rainbow. A sign was added to the promise, exhibiting the wonderful goodness of God. He uses such signs as a means of confirming our faith in his word, as with the sacraments. The rainbow became a seal of assurance of God's promise. This covenant went from specific to general, from people who understand to living creatures and the earth, who do not understand. However, the covenant was addressed to Noah and his posterity, who by faith were able to understand the promise. Each covenant sign God gave was appropriate to its context. Circumcision was for each male, marking him as a member of the people of God, who in turn became the spiritual head of his household. It was applied to the individual. However, the rainbow sign applied not just to people but to the earth and all that was in it. Therefore, it "covers" all to which it applies by stretching across the sky with people, animals, and earth beneath.

It is significant that this covenantal sign was made with every living creature and the earth itself so they could be preserved. Isn't it interesting that God wanted to preserve the continuance of animal and plant life instead of unrepentant human beings? If God so esteems his creation and has given it to us for our dominion, we should do all we can to preserve and protect it for future generations to enjoy. God is Lord over the whole world, and all his creation glorifies him. "The earth is the LORD's, and everything in it, the world, and all who live in it" (Ps. 24:1). God preserves the world, for it is his throne. If this is God's world, then how should we live in it? Since we have been given dominion over it, we must make conscious efforts at protecting wildlife, avoiding destruction or the overuse of nonrenewable resources, and protecting the environment from destructive pollution. Suburban sprawl that does not protect trees, wildlife, groundwater, and streams needs to be brought under control. Overfishing and polluting the world's oceans should be stopped. All need to do his or her part and efforts made on a collective level through local, state, and national governments. The beauty and wonder of the diversity of creation should aid in our worship of God. All creation, from the sun, moon, stars, sea creatures, stormy winds, mountains, and fruit trees to wild animals, birds, kings, nations, and children are all to praise the Lord (Ps. 148). So when we see a rainbow, let's remember it is not only a promise to us but also to all the earth that it may be preserved for God's glorious praise.

A rainbow is "the arc containing the colors of the spectrum in consecutive bands, formed in the sky by the refraction, reflection and dispersion of the sun's rays in falling rain or in mist."[3] It is not seen in every storm cloud, but it reminds the LORD of his promise. We in turn should be reminded of God's gracious covenant with us.

How can we look at a rainbow and not be awed by its beauty? When we see that beauty, we are reminded of God's covenant love for all his creatures and the earth. We also remember that though "the creation was subjected to frustration," we have a "hope that the creation itself will be liberated from its bondage to decay and brought into the glorious freedom of the children of God" (Rom. 8:20, 21).

People often ask, "Was this the first time a rainbow ever appeared?" We are not told directly the answer to this in the text. Numerous commentators think the rainbow was not a new phenomenon but simply had a new significance attached to it.[4] Francis Schaeffer says this is possible, since both circumcision and baptism were not new rites but were given new meaning from God as covenantal signs.[5] Some see the rainbow's appearance after the Flood as a sign of the covenant necessarily implied this was when it first appeared. However, we have no way to prove this one way or another. To the frightened survivors of the Flood, seeing a rainbow for the first time would have had a more significant impact and reassuring effect that this was God's promise of withholding his further judgment. But the impact may have been simply the special revelation of the significance of the covenant sign.

If it were the first appearance of the rainbow, does that mean it never rained before the Flood? Some have taken this view. When the LORD God made the earth and heavens before he made humans, "no shrub of the field had yet appeared on the earth and no plant of the field had yet sprung up, for the LORD God had not sent rain on the earth and there was no man to work the ground, but streams [or mist] came up from the earth and watered the whole surface of the ground" (Gen. 2:5, 6). Then the LORD planted a garden in Eden out of which flowed a river that watered the garden (Gen. 2:8, 10). No further mention is made of rain until the Flood. "On that day all the springs of the great deep burst forth, and the floodgates of the heavens were opened. And rain fell on the earth forty days and forty nights" (Gen. 7:11, 12). From this description and the fact that there was continual rain all over the earth for forty days and nights indicate that different atmospheric conditions existed prior to the Flood. Possibly the earth was covered with a thick vapor canopy. Some have thought that this may account for the longevity of the people described in Genesis 5, some of whom lived over nine hundred years. The vapor canopy would have blocked harmful ultraviolet rays that would shorten their lifespans.

Many of those who hold to the view of a universal Flood believe the atmosphere was different before the Flood than after it. Although seasons are mentioned at the initial creation (Gen. 1:14), could not God's promise that "seedtime and harvest, cold and heat, summer and winter" would never cease (Gen. 8:22) indicate a new situation after the Flood? Some see possible evidence of this with the thousands of woolly mammoths and other animals found living among heavy vegetation in what are today icy polar regions. In fact, complete mammoths have been found frozen with plants in their mouths and stomachs that can still be identified. While building a road in Siberia, workmen discovered a subterranean frozen river with ancient fish that had been frozen while still swimming in midstream. The workmen ate the fish.[6] These instant deep freezes thousands of years ago indicate a sudden change in climate that may be accounted for by the cataclysmic events of the Flood. All this is said to point to the possibility that the first rainbow appeared after the Flood as a sign of God's covenant. The new atmospheric and groundwater conditions after the Flood would prevent a similar universal flood from ever occurring again.

As I have described previously, uniformitarians discredit these explanations and say that rain has been falling for probably millions of years. But how can the "no rain" of Genesis 2:5, 6 then be explained? These verses are in the second description of creation, which gives different details than Genesis 1. No rain occurred at the early stage of creation, so plant life was not yet created either (Gen. 2:5). Then the LORD planted a garden in which he put Adam. Presumably, rain followed, allowing for the development of agriculture and the raising of livestock (Gen. 4:2, 20). Rather than introducing a new thing, the covenantal promise of the continuance of the seasons was part of the many aspects of repetition of the creation events (Gen. 1:14; cf. Ps. 104:19) in the re-creation after the Flood.

If the earth had been covered with a canopy of cloud, how could the sun, moon, and stars have been seen before the flood? Obviously, they could not have been. But at creation we are told that they were given by God on the fourth day to "serve as signs to mark seasons and days and years . . . to give light on the earth . . . to govern the day and the night" (Gen. 1:14–18). Would not suddenly seeing them have been a greater sign to Noah than a rainbow? What was natural in the appearance of a rainbow before the flood was the same afterwards. But God instituted the rainbow as a sign and seal of his promises.

The fact that a rainbow is formed by the interaction of light, air, and water as clouds begin to dissipate is no proof that it was not an act of God's doing. God makes the laws of nature, and they have their purposes within his plan for the universe. He uses both nature and grace to accomplish his purposes for our lives, and he gives it all its meaning. With our eyes, we see that it may affect our hearts and confirm our faith.

∼ The Significance of the Sign

What does the sign of the rainbow mean? In this sign, God gives us simple reassurance that we are not about to be destroyed by a universal flood again. As the LORD responded to Job from the storm, he let him know that he controls the fall of rain and the boundaries of the sea (Job 38:8–11). Nothing is beyond his controlling power. God's plan is for the earth to be filled with his creation of both people and animals. He receives honor and glory through this fulfillment of his purpose. As the rainbow spreads out between heaven and earth, it proclaims a temporal peace between God and humanity.

In spreading its arc across the whole horizon, it teaches us the universal nature of God's common grace.[7]

Although it is not explicit, some scholars, such as von Rad and Witsius, have seen in the rainbow an image of God's laid aside upside-down battle bow pointing to heaven as an end to his war on humanity. It is a sign of comfort, not terror. The Psalms use the imagery of bolts of lightning being God's arrows (Ps. 18:14). Thus, the sun coming out at the end of a storm indicates God's mercy in judgment. The resulting rainbow out of the gloomy cloud is a token of God's grace.[8] The seal of God's "covenant with Noah emphasizes the gracious character of this covenant."[9] Through the destructive forces of the storm clouds shines the beautiful light spectrum of the sun's rays illustrating the mercy of divine grace delivering us from judgment.

DeJong sees in the circle of the rainbow[10] God's wedding band as a reminder to himself that we have been married to him. We are his bride, and Christ is our groom (Matt. 25:1–13; Eph. 5:25; Rev. 19:9). Referring again to Isaiah 54, we see the connection Isaiah made between marriage and God's covenant with Noah. The LORD said to Israel,

> "For your Maker is your husband—
>   the LORD Almighty is his name—
> the Holy One of Israel is your Redeemer;
>   he is called the God of all the earth. . . .
> To me this is like the days of Noah,
>   when I swore that the waters of Noah would never again cover
>   the earth.
> So now I have sworn not to be angry with you,
>   never to rebuke you again.
> Though the mountains be shaken
> and the hills be removed,
>   yet my unfailing love for you will not be shaken
>   nor my covenant of peace be removed,"
>   says the LORD, who has compassion on you." (Isa. 54:5, 9, 10)

If Israel were the LORD's bride and he made a covenant of peace with her that reminded him of his covenant with Noah, then the sign of that covenant, the rainbow, took on the meaning roughly equivalent to a wedding band. As wearing a wedding band reminds us that we are in a marriage covenant, the rainbow reminds God of his covenant love for us and all life on the earth. Twice God repeats, "I will remember" (Gen. 9:15, 16). The rainbow is a never-ending circle reminding God that he is married to us and to his creation.

God desires to make known his goodness to his creatures. The rainbow provides such a testimony. The universal character of God's covenant with Noah, testified by the rainbow seen around the world, provides a foundation for the gospel to be proclaimed to all nations and peoples. As the rainbow confirmed the Noahic covenant, its continuance is seen in the maintenance of the seasons and days throughout history, telling us of God's patience toward all humanity. The skies "proclaim the work of his hands," speak with a voice heard in every language, and go "out into all the earth" (Ps. 19:1–4).

Barnabas and Paul picked up this theme in preaching to the crowd at Lystra saying,

> "We are bringing you good news, telling you to turn from these worthless things [false gods] to the living God, who made heaven and earth and sea and everything in them. In the past, he let all nations go their own way. Yet he has not left himself without testimony: He has shown kindness by giving you rain from heaven and crops in their seasons; he provides you with plenty of food and fills your hearts with joy." (Acts 14:15–17)

The goodness of God seen in his general revelation and common grace to all forms a basis for testifying to the special grace found in the gospel of Christ to the whole world. Paul emphasized this point in his argument to the Romans when he quoted Psalm 19:4 in Romans 10:18. The Israelites were without excuse for not having heard the message of God for the skies have proclaimed his message to the ends of the world. We, too, have that message as a platform to proclaim Jesus as "Lord of all" and the one who "richly blesses all who call on him" (Rom. 10:12). May we remember to use the rainbow as a testimony of God's faithfulness and goodness to all until sin is no more.

⌇ God Revealed in the Bow

The number seven in the colors of the rainbow is the number of perfection, illustrating the perfection and beauty of God. It is an anthropomorphic expression of the presence of God and his grace toward all his creation. Since the rainbow is a reflection of the sun's rays on the mist in the sky, so we should see the sign of the covenant as deriving from Christ the "sun of righteousness" (Mal. 4:2; cf. Luke 1:78).

The vision of God and Christ seen in the rainbow or something like it is used four times in Scripture. First, as Moses and Aaron, along with the elders of Israel, confirmed the covenant with the LORD, they saw a vision of God in which "under his feet was something like a pavement made of sapphire, clear as the sky itself" (Exod. 24:10). The picture of the beautiful gem shimmering from the LORD's glory is expanded in other visions of him.

Second, in the vision given to the apostle John, he saw a door open in heaven and heard a voice saying to come up to see what was to come. "At once I was in the Spirit, and there before me was a throne in heaven with someone sitting on it. And the one who sat there had the appearance of jasper and carnelian. A rainbow, resembling an emerald, encircled the throne" (Rev. 4:3). This pictures God ruling from his throne of power and dominion. Since God "lives in unapproachable light, whom no one has seen or can see" (1 Tim. 6:16), he is described in terms of light reflecting off clear blue sapphire, jasper (green quartz), and carnelian (red chalcedony) stones. An emerald (transparent bright green) rainbow encircles his throne.

Third, John's vision was somewhat similar to the vision the prophet Ezekiel saw while with exiled Judah in Babylon. Ezekiel said, "I looked, and I saw a windstorm coming out of the north—an immense cloud with flashing lightning and surrounded by brilliant light" (Ezek. 1:4). In the center of a fire, he saw four unusual looking living creatures.

> Then there came a voice from above the expanse over their heads as [the four creatures] stood with lowered wings. Above the expanse over their heads was what looked like a throne of sapphire, and high above on the throne was a figure like that of a man. I saw that from what appeared to be his waist up he looked like glowing metal, as if full of fire, and that from there down he looked like fire; and brilliant light surrounded him. Like the appearance of a rainbow in the clouds on a rainy day, so was the radiance around him.
>
> This was the appearance of the likeness of the glory of the LORD. When I saw it, I fell facedown, and I heard the voice of one speaking. (Ezek. 1:25–28)

The expanse over the heads of the creatures separated them from the glory of the LORD. The prophet Ezekiel had a vision of the glory of the LORD symbolically revealed, without seeing God directly. Note that the brilliant light around the figure looked like a rainbow, with lightning flashing in an immense cloud in the background.

Both John's and Ezekiel's visions used the image of a brilliant rainbow to describe God's awesome glory, beauty, holiness, power, and presence. When we meditate on these things, we see our own smallness, weakness, and sinfulness.

What a wonderful reminder God has given that he is truly here for us. He has not left us alone in the world. Nor did he, as deists believe, create the world, wind it up like a clock, and leave it to run on its own. Each appearance of the rainbow reminds us that God is intimately involved with our world. He is watching us and is concerned with what we are doing with our lives. Are we living for him? Have we repented from our sins? We are accountable to him for how we live our lives.

Although God promised he would not destroy the earth again by flood, does that mean he will not destroy it by some other means? Peter warned us that the world is reserved for judgment by fire next time even though it seems that "everything goes on as it has since the beginning of creation." He said, "By these waters also the world of that time was deluged and destroyed. By the same word the present heavens and earth are reserved for fire, being kept for the day of judgment and destruction of ungodly men" (2 Pet. 3:4, 6, 7).

Fourth, later in John's vision in Revelation, he saw a mighty angel, perhaps Jesus Christ, coming down from heaven "robed in a cloud, with a rainbow above his head; his face was like the sun, and his legs were like fiery pillars" (Rev. 10:1). This angel, with a loud voice like seven thunders, announced a coming divine judgment on those who refuse God's love and grace. The rainbow above his head brought a reminder of God's stay of judgment for all these ages since the Flood. Peter expressed God's forbearance: "He is patient with you, not wanting anyone to perish, but everyone to come to repentance" (2 Pet. 3:9). God has not brought his judgment on us yet because he is still waiting for us to come to faith and repentance, if we have not yet done so. We must trust in him now while we still have time.

⁓ A Cause for Praise

Don't let the rainbow flags and window stickers, which distort the truth, distract us from the real significance of God's rainbow. The next time we see a rainbow, we should reflect on God's deliverance from judgment and patience in waiting for our repentance. May we be comforted in seeing God's goodness toward all his creation and awed in meditating on his beauty in holiness. As the LORD said to Noah, "I will remember my covenant between me and you and all living creatures of every kind" (Gen. 9:15). May we glorify God for remembering his covenant and forgetting our sins (Jer. 31:34). In his mercy, he does not deal with us according to our sins. In his covenant, he promised no more destruction of the earth by flood, and he has kept that promise.

The vision God has given us for the future of the renewed world is glorious. Rather than being filled with corruption and violence, the earth will be filled with righteousness, peace, and love. The wicked will be wiped away, and the prince of this world will be sent to destruction. A great flood of a different nature will break over the earth. "For the earth will be filled with the knowledge of the glory of the LORD, as the waters cover the sea" (Hab. 2:14; cf. Isa. 11:9).

Psalm 33 could have appropriately fit the praise that Noah and his family must have given to the LORD as they worshiped at the altar Noah built. Perhaps they sang such a new song, celebrating God's saving acts as they saw the covenantal rainbow as a sign that God would no longer destroy the earth by flood.

> Sing to him a new song;
>> play skillfully, and shout for joy.
> For the word of the LORD is right and true;
>> he is faithful in all he does.
> The LORD loves righteousness and justice;
>> the earth is full of his unfailing love.
> By the word of the LORD were the heavens made,
>> their starry host by the breath of his mouth.
> He gathers the waters of the sea into jars;
>> he puts the deep into storehouses.
> Let all the earth fear the LORD;
>> let all the people of the world revere him.
> For he spoke, and it came to be;
>> he commanded, and it stood firm.

The LORD foils the plans of the nations;
> he thwarts the purposes of the peoples.
But the plans of the LORD stand firm forever,
> the purposes of his heart through all generations. (Ps. 33:3–11)

Noah, whose name sounds like the Hebrew for comfort, was a comfort to those faithful to the LORD due to the curse on the ground in whom there was hope of a rest from our painful toil in the promised one (Gen. 5:29). As God worked through righteous Noah, he brought comfort to humankind, assuring them there would no longer be judgment on the earth through a worldwide flood. God continues to remember his covenant with us as he sees the rainbow. For that we can thank and praise the LORD. As Matthew Henry said, "Let us give him the glory of his mercy in promising, and truth in performing."[11] Let us make known among the nations of the earth the judgments, power, and mercy of our God. Then may all peoples acknowledge how great our awesome God is and proclaim that his name is exalted. God's covenant of common grace, mercy, and comfort, as seen universally in the rainbow, reminds the world of who he is and who we are in relation to him. As he never forgets his covenant promises to us, may we never forget to acknowledge him in all things. May the LORD use us to lead the spiritually blind to have eyes of faith to understand his truth as seen in creation and interpreted for our redemption in his Word.

God's common-grace covenant with Noah prepared the world stage for a renewed program of the redemptive covenant as it was later revealed to Abraham. The common-grace covenant reestablished the universal witness of general revelation of God's eternal power, kindness, and patience toward us to lead us to repentance (Rom. 1:20; 2:4, 5; 2 Pet. 3:9). This has prepared the world for the second universal witness of special revelation, the "word of Christ" (Rom. 10:17) so that peoples of all nations may find blessing through the messianic Seed of Abraham.[12]

SCRIPTURE READING:

REVELATION 4

Discussion Questions

1. What type of covenant sign was the rainbow?
2. What is the significance of the rainbow after the Flood?
3. What does the rainbow display to us about God?
4. What kind of relationship does the rainbow remind God that he has made with us?
5. What significance may we find in God making his covenant with every living creature and the earth? Should that adjust how we treat them?
6. How may we use the rainbow as a foundation for our witness to the gospel?
7. In light of God's staying of his judgment by flood and the promise of destruction by fire yet to come, how should we live today?
8. Why is God still patiently waiting (cf. Rom. 2:4; 2 Pet. 3:9)?
9. What place does the common-grace covenant have in preparing people for God's redemptive covenant through the "word of Christ"?

Notes

1. O.V. Gerlach as quoted in C. F. Keil and F. Delitzsch, *Commentary on the Old Testament*, vol. 1 (Grand Rapids: Eerdmans, 1975), 154.

2. Geerhardus Vos, *Biblical Theology* (Grand Rapids: Eerdmans, 1948), 66.

3. David B. Guralnik, ed., *Webster's New World Dictionary of the American Language*, 2nd ed. (Cleveland: Collins, 1979), 1173.

4. See Matthew Henry, *An Exposition of the Old and New Testament*, Vol. 1 (Philadelphia: Towar, J. & D. M. Hogan, 1830), 76; Herman Witsius, *The Economy of the Covenants between God and Man*, Vol. 2 (Reprint, Kingsburg, Calif.: den Dulk Christian Foundation, 1990) 241; Oswald T. Allis, *God Spake by Moses* (Nutley, N.J.: Presbyterian and Reformed, 1958), 25; Vos, *Biblical Theology*, 66–67.

5. Francis A. Schaeffer, *Genesis in Space and Time: The Flow of Biblical History* (Downers Grove, Ill.: InterVarsity Press, 1972), 148.

6. Walt Brown, *In the Beginning: Compelling Evidence for Creation and the Flood*, 7th ed. (Phoenix, Ariz.: Center for Scientific Creation, 2001), 170.

7. Keil and Delitzsch, *Commentary on the Old Testament*, 155.

8. Derek Kidner, *Genesis*, vol. 1 of *The Tyndale Old Testament Commentaries* (Downers Grove, Ill.: InterVarsity, 1967), 102.

9. O. Palmer Robertson, *The Christ of the Covenants* (Phillipsburg, N.J.: Presbyterian and Reformed, 1980), 123.

10. A complete rainbow circle may be seen by flying over a storm in an airplane. From the earth we can only see the rainbow extend from one end of the horizon to the other. When the sun is at an angle of greater than 42 degrees, the rainbow cannot be seen at all. Norman DeJong, *God's Wedding Band* (Winamac, Ind.: Redeemer Books, 1990), 57.

11. Matthew Henry, *An Exposition of the Old and New Testaments.* Vol. 1 (Philadelphia: Towar, J. & D. M. Hogan, 1830), 75.

12. Meredith G. Kline, *Kingdom Prologue* (Overland Park, Kans.: Two Age Press, 2000), 261–262.

Noah and His Three Sons

Genesis 9:18–29

18 *The sons of Noah who came out of the ark were Shem, Ham and Japheth. (Ham was the father of Canaan.)* **19** *These were the three sons of Noah, and from them came the people who were scattered over the earth.*

    20 *Noah, a man of the soil, proceeded to plant a vineyard.* **21** *When he drank some of its wine, he became drunk and lay uncovered inside his tent.* **22** *Ham, the father of Canaan, saw his father's nakedness and told his two brothers outside.* **23** *But Shem and Japheth took a garment and laid it across their shoulders; then they walked in backward and covered their father's nakedness. Their faces were turned the other way so that they would not see their father's nakedness.*

    24 *When Noah awoke from his wine and found out what his youngest son had done to him,* **25** *He said,*

"Cursed be Canaan!
The lowest of slaves
will he be to his brothers."

26 *He also said,*

"Blessed be the LORD, the God of Shem!
May Canaan be the slave of Shem.
27 *May God extend the territory of Japheth;*
may Japheth live in the tents of Shem,
and may Canaan be his slave."
28 *After the flood Noah lived 350 years.* **29** *Altogether,*
Noah lived 950 years, and then he died.

WE ARE NOW introduced to a closing section on the life of Noah after the giving of the covenant signified by the rainbow. "The sons of Noah who came out of the ark were Shem, Ham and Japheth" (Gen. 9:18). Actually, Japheth was the oldest (Gen. 10:21) and Ham the youngest (Gen. 9:24). Shem was mentioned first as the father of the blessed godly line through whom the Redeemer promised to Eve was to be born. Ham was mentioned second, since his descendants played a prominent role through biblical history in their relationship with the Semites. From these three sons came all the peoples of the earth who were scattered over it. Although Noah lived 350 years more after the Flood (v. 28), he had no other children. This is a prologue to the widespread description of nations in chapter 10. Verses 25–27 describing the curses and blessings on Noah's descendants narrows the focus down to the godly line of Shem, which begins in chapter 11, verse 10.

Continuing the model of showing the coming out of the ark and the start of a new beginning as paralleling the creation account, this passage also illustrated numerous parallels. Just as God planted a garden for people to enjoy, Noah planted a vineyard. As Adam and Eve ate the fruit in the Garden of Eden and were naked, Noah ate of the fruit of his vineyard and exposed his nakedness. For both, the effect of their sin was nakedness. As Adam had sinned, so Noah sinned. The effect of their sins was felt for the generations that followed. Even though righteous Noah and his family were saved from God's judgment on sin that had corrupted the human race, that corruption was still inherent in all people. A deep division continued between the people of God and the people of Satan, those in the light and those in darkness.

∼ Noah's Drunkenness

The next events concerning Noah's life may have happened some decades after the Flood. Ham already had four sons, with Canaan, his youngest, probably at least of accountable age.

Noah, a man of the soil, was a farmer. He planted a vineyard and drank the wine produced from it. Although this is the first mention of wine in the Bible, it may have been available since the days of Cain when he "brought some of the fruits of the soil as an offering to the LORD" (Gen. 4:3). Wine was depicted in both negative and positive ways throughout the Scriptures. When it was abused, as Noah did, it was a curse and a cause for much sin. When it was used in moderation, it was a blessing and a cause for rejoicing. In describing God's blessings, the psalmist spoke of "wine that gladdens the heart of man" (Ps. 104:15). Jesus' first miracle was to make more wine at the wedding feast of Cana (John 2:1–11). Wine was used at the Passover Feast and is used to represent the blood of Christ at the Lord's Supper. However, let us beware of seeking to bury our sorrows and troubles by drinking too much. Proverbs warned us,

> Who has woe? Who has sorrow?
> Who has strife? Who has complaints?
> Who has needless bruises? Who has bloodshot eyes?

Those who linger over wine,
  who go to sample bowls of mixed wine.
Do not gaze at wine when it is red,
  when it sparkles in the cup,
  when it goes down smoothly!
In the end it bites like a snake
  and poisons like a viper.
Your eyes will see strange sights
  and your mind imagine confusing things. (Prov. 23:29–33)

Noah may have been depressed after his initial high in rejoicing and worshiping God after being saved through the Flood. The whole world had been wiped out so only he and his family were left. It must have been lonely with the world practically empty. But most likely family strife was already present. Perhaps to drown his sorrows, he overindulged in an intoxicating drink. However, this was the wrong approach to take. He should have sought refuge in the LORD. By lying drunk and naked in his tent, Noah lost his decency and honor. We are reminded of Satan's deceptive work in the garden when Adam and Eve discovered their own nakedness through their fall into sin. Although with the end of the Flood there was a "new creation," people's sinful natures had not changed. Noah had fallen into sin.

Although we have lived upright and good lives, we always face the danger of falling into sin, even in our old age. We must always be on our guard. As Charles Erdman comments, "How evident it is that neither rich experience nor the wisdom of old age make one immune from the assault of evil. . . . It is also true that neither memories, however tragic or sacred, nor responsibilities, however great, can keep one from sin."[1] Most of us are familiar with the sinful failures of some who have been great church leaders. Let us beware!

Noah, a "preacher of righteousness" (2 Pet. 2:5), "was a righteous man, blameless among the people of his time, and he walked with God" (Gen. 6:9). As a man of great faith, he was commended more highly than almost any others in the Scriptures. But the Bible does not hide the sins of its heroes of faith. This fact points to the authorship of the Scriptures being from God. If it were simply a human book, an effort would have been made to ignore, conceal, or give excuses for his sin. But truthful pictures of the characters of the Bible are given to us to show the reality of our fallen condition and our need for the grace of God. Throughout the Bible, we are shown that "all have sinned and fall short of the glory of God" (Rom. 3:23). If Noah could fall into sin, so can anyone of us. Paul warned us, "So, if you think you are standing firm, be careful that you don't fall!" (1 Cor. 10:12). It is sad to see how after living a righteous life for 601 years, Noah had a major fall. A number of persons in the Bible who began strong in following the LORD while young departed from living for him when older (e.g., Lot, Eli, and Solomon). This is evidence that our past walk with God does not provide power for future victory if we neglect our relationship with him. We must seek and praise the Lord daily (Ps. 96:2). To be a blessed people, we must delight "in the law of the LORD, and on his law" meditate "day and night" (Ps. 1:2; cf. 119:97). With the psalmist, may we say, "My heart is set on keeping your decrees to the very end" (Ps. 119:112).

None of us ever comes to the point in our lives when we no longer are tempted or we don't need God's sustaining grace. Paul warned us, "Be careful that you don't fall!" (1 Cor. 10:12). We can never stand in our own strength, but only by faith (2 Cor. 1:24). "It is God who makes . . . us . . . stand firm in Christ" (2 Cor. 1:21). We cannot sing with the hymn, "Lord, we are able." Rather, when we realize we are *not* able, we learn to lean on Christ alone to fight our spiritual battles against temptation and Satan.[2] Then we can pray as our Lord taught us, "And lead us not into temptation, but deliver us from the evil one" (Matt. 6:13). He will not allow us to be tempted beyond what we are able to bear but will provide a way out (1 Cor. 10:13).

∽ Ham's Shamelessness

"Ham, the father of Canaan, saw his father's nakedness and told his two brothers outside" (Gen. 9:22). Exactly what sin did Ham commit that led to Noah cursing his grandson Canaan? Numerous interpretations have been made concerning the meaning of this verse. Some have thought it said in an obscure way that Ham revealed the nakedness of his father's wife and had an incestuous relationship with her, with Canaan being the offspring of that union. But it does not make sense that he would then tell his two brothers outside the tent. The rabbis taught that Ham had castrated his father, thus explaining why he had no more sons. But it was not that Ham became sexually involved, for the text tells us, "Ham . . . saw his father's nakedness." If Ham had become involved sexually, the Hebrew text would be translated that "he uncovered his father's nakedness." But Noah had already uncovered himself (Gen. 9:21).[3]

Whatever may have actually happened is not the main point; rather, it is the contrast in response to the situation between Ham and his two brothers. Apparently, Ham did not just stumble into the tent and happen to see his father drunk and naked. He could have modestly covered his father. But to gaze at another's nakedness in either lust or scorn is morally wrong. Rather than being restrained by reverence for his father, Ham stared at his nakedness.

Prior to Adam and Eve's fall in the garden, they felt no shame when naked. But after the Fall, they lost their innocence and felt their shame. Nakedness suggests weakness, need, and humiliation. In our nakedness, we recognize our moral frailty, our tendency toward the lusts of the flesh. God's redemption for humanity was connected with his providing a covering for sin, which was symbolized by his provision of animal skin coverings for Adam and Eve (Gen. 3:21).

Ham's scornful leering at his father rather than revering him was reprehensible. In ancient times, "seeing one's father naked was a breach of family ethic. The sanctity of the family was destroyed and the strength of the father was made a mockery."[4] In not covering his father's shame and then gleefully telling his brothers of their father's degradation, Ham was doing an exceedingly unfilial act. Rather than honoring his father, he exposed his sin. Apparently, Ham was a rebellious son who did not share his father's faith. When he finally found his father in sin, he gloated in his parent's failure, and he sought the camaraderie of his brothers with this attitude. His exulting in this was "as if he had triumphed over his father."[5] Such a dishonoring of one's parents is strongly condemned in Mosaic Law. Anyone who struck or cursed his father or mother or was stubborn and rebellious was put to death (Exod. 21:15, 17; Deut. 21:18–21; cf. Mark 7:10). Those who exult in shame are true sons of Ham.

Ham was doing the opposite of the fifth commandment, which says, "Honor your father and your mother, so that you may live long in the land the LORD your God is giving you" (Exod. 20:12). To honor means to prize highly, care for, show respect for, and obey. Only by honoring our fathers and mothers can we uphold God's delegated authority over us. By so doing, we will receive his blessing.

It appears to some that Ham may have attempted to seize leadership over his brothers for his own family line. But his attempt failed.[6] Ham's exulting in his father's shame and attempt to usurp authority led to the marring of his inheritance through a curse. Thus, Canaan was not placed in leadership but was subservient to his relatives.

In contrast to Ham's response to his father's shameful nakedness, "Shem and Japheth took a garment and laid it across their shoulders; then they walked in backward and covered their father's nakedness. Their faces were turned the other way so that they would not see their father's nakedness" (Gen. 9:23). This was the most honorable thing they could do in that situation. It indicated their desire to imitate God, as he had clothed our naked first parents in the Garden of Eden. Their action was a type of the gracious work of Christ done for us while we were in our sin and shame. Jesus hung naked on the cross (Matt. 27:35), bearing our sin (1 John 1:7), and scorning its shame (Heb. 12:2). His atonement on the cross covers our nakedness and shame. We are no longer guilty and under condemnation (Rom. 8:1), but by faith we are now clothed in the clean white robes of righteousness, making us fit for the wedding banquet of the Lamb of God at the end of the age (cf. Matt. 22:11–14; Rev. 7:14). The Lamb who takes away the sin of the world (John 1:29) washes us clean so we are "without stain or wrinkle or any other blemish, but holy and blameless" (Eph. 5:27).

Noah did not remain in his life of sin, for it had been graciously covered. "Love covers over a multitude of sins" (1 Pet. 4:8). Upon awaking, he took the role of a prophet, speaking by the Spirit of God.

∽ Canaan's Curse

After Noah's fall into drunkenness, through grace he received another opportunity to be God's spokesperson. Noah's sin became the occasion for the LORD's prophecy concerning his descendants. Noah now realized the injunction of Paul, "Do not get drunk on wine, which leads to debauchery. Instead, be filled with the Spirit" (Eph. 5:18). He then proclaimed the will and word of God. When he awoke from his wine and found out what his youngest son had done to him, he said,

> "Cursed be Canaan!
> The lowest of slaves
> will he be to his brothers." (Gen. 9:25)

Since Noah's blessings and curses were directed at the descendants of his three sons, it was natural that he named Canaan as the one cursed. Noah's three sons, including Ham, had already been blessed (Gen. 9:1).

Ham was Noah's youngest son (Gen. 9:24), and Canaan was Ham's youngest of four sons (10:6). Twice we are told that Ham was the father of Canaan (9:18, 22) in anticipation of the connection between Ham's sin and the curse on his son. The emphasis was on Ham's progeny rather than on Ham. Canaan was not punished for something his father did, but the sins of fathers are continued in their descendants. The emphasis made in the passage by repeating that Canaan was Ham's son, especially where Ham's offensive behavior was described (9:22), seems to indicate that Canaan shared his father's rejection of Noah's faith and Ham's defiant attitude. Noah did not just curse Canaan but the nations who would descend from Canaan. For having brought rupture in the family, Ham's own family would suffer the consequences. This was retributive justice. As God said to the Israelites in giving the Ten Commandments, ". . . for I, the LORD your God, am a jealous God, punishing the children for the sin of the fathers to the third and fourth generation of those who hate me" (Exod. 20:5). Thus, we see the terrible consequences our sins can have on subsequent generations. Often children, grandchildren, and great-grandchildren repeat the sins of their forefathers. In biblical times, this many generations usually lived in one household.

It was only one branch of the Hamites, the Canaanites, who were specifically cursed. This family group in a particular way would be recipients of God's curse, although the curse may have had wider application to other branches of Ham's descendants. But no connection was made with the Negroid race. In Noah's curse, he made a prophecy, a prediction as to what would happen to Canaan's descendants. "The lowest of slaves will he be to his brothers" (Gen. 9:25). Foretelling the future is not an injustice. In spiritual terms, Canaan would be reprobate, one who was separated from the blessings of God. Satan's seed, seen in Canaan's family line, would be defeated by the Seed of the woman seen in Shem's family line. Noah made a wordplay with Canaan's name, for the root *kanaʿ*

signifies subjugation. Noah's curse found its ultimate fulfillment in Israel's conquest of Canaan (Deut. 9:3; Judg. 4:23).[7]

The servitude of Canaan's descendants was due to their degraded lives of sin. It may be that the fulfillment of this curse on Canaan was first fulfilled when his descendants in Palestine were subject for twelve years to Kedorlaomer, king of Elam. When they rebelled, four eastern kings, descendants of Shem, conquered five kings, descendants of Ham, including the kings of Sodom and Gomorrah (Gen. 14:1–11). These Canaanite cities were particularly known for their immorality and neglect of the poor. (However, Abram rescued Lot who had been taken captive with the king of Sodom and in the process, defeated the eastern kings.) The fulfillment of Noah's prophecy also may have been completed with the Gibeonites, descendants of Canaan, being forced to be woodcutters and water carriers for the entire Israelite community when Joshua conquered the land of Canaan (Josh. 9:23). Later, the Ephraimites did not dislodge the Canaanites in Gezer but required them to do forced labor (Josh. 16:10). Also concerning Canaan's descendants under King Solomon's rule, "All the people left from the Amorites, Hittites, Perizzites, Hivites and Jebusites (these peoples were not Israelites), that is, their descendants remaining in the land, whom the Israelites could not exterminate—these Solomon conscripted for his slave labor force" (1 Kings 9:20, 21). These principles of curse and blessing are generally seen today. In countries where corruption, immorality, and disregard for authority and the rule of law are rampant, a curse appears to be on much of the land. Usually, these people are poor and in servitude or debt to those countries that uphold God's laws.

We see in Ham's malicious disrespect an allusion to the entrance again of Satan's seed to destroy the faithful remnant family. Through the faithful line of Seth down to Noah, the promise of a Redeemer for humanity remained. In the cursing of Canaan and his descendants, a curse was put on those nonelect who despised God's promise that he would send a Savior for humankind. The curse on

Canaan must be understood in spiritual terms as part of God's judgment on Satan.

The disposition of Ham toward immorality and disrespect for family relations bore fruit in the immorality of his Canaanite descendants. God gave the Israelites commandments regarding sexual behavior and said, "You must not do as they do in Egypt, where you used to live, and you must not do as they do in the land of Canaan, where I am bringing you. Do not follow their practices" (Lev. 18:3). God then proceeded to give laws against incest, adultery, homosexuality, and bestiality. The Canaanites also became wicked idolaters who sacrificed their children on altars of fire (Lev. 18:21; 2 Kings 16:3). God strongly warned the Israelites against mixing with these people. Through intermarriage between the Israelites and the Canaanites, Satan attempted to destroy God's blessing and the coming of the Redeemer. But God brought judgment on those Israelites who did not remain faithful. Many Canaanite nations were eventually destroyed by Israel, who were Semites, as they conquered the land of Canaan. God said that because of these sins, the land became defiled and would vomit out its people (Lev. 18:25). God brought judgment on them through the Israelite conquest because of their grievous sins in the pattern of their forefather Ham.

Historian and Bible scholar Howard Vos said,

> Whatever the curse was, it was on Canaan, not Ham. And whatever it was, it has been fulfilled because the Canaanites have passed from history. And the curse seems to have been moral rather than ethnic or physical. The Canaanites were a morally debased people, but culturally they were sometimes fairly advanced and had much to teach the Israelites and others.[8]

Judging by the peoples descended from Canaan, we can clearly see that he was a Caucasian. Therefore, there is no basis for the view promoted by racists at the height of slavery in the nineteenth century that black Africans were eternally cursed to slavery because they are descendants of Ham. This strange teaching was the single greatest justification for Black slavery for more than a thousand years, although it makes no reference to Blacks at all. It was used to justify the consciences of many Christians who owned slaves. The universal association of black and white with evil and goodness, and sin and purity has led to perceptions, symbolic associations, and historical ramifications of Black enslavement.[9]

Any attempt to divide the world by race or ethnicity today based on Genesis 9:25–27 is totally contrary to New Testament teaching that says, "There is no Greek or Jew . . . barbarian, Scythian, slave or free, but Christ is all, and is in all" (Col. 3:11). Today no barrier wall of partition exists between Jew and Gentile in the kingdom of God (Eph. 2:14). The Holy Spirit has revealed that the mystery of Christ "is that through the gospel the Gentiles are heirs together with Israel, members together of one body, and sharers together in the promise in Christ Jesus" (Eph. 3:6). We are all one people, one family in Christ.

Finally, the negative example of Ham and Canaan illustrates for us the dangerous consequences of apostasy, of having once shared in the blessings of the covenant community, of being enlightened, tasting the life of faith, tasting the goodness of the Word of God, and seeing the power of the Holy Spirit (Heb. 6:4, 5). Ham experienced all this in the Flood event and in the ministry of his father Noah. It is similar to people who have been baptized and attend church but demonstrate no spiritual fruit in their lives. God warns us, "But land that produces thorns and thistles is worthless and is in danger of being cursed. In the end it will be burned" (Heb. 6:8). The fruit in their lives demonstrates the true state of their hearts and whether they produce the "things that accompany salvation" (Heb. 6:9).

∼ Shem's and Japheth's Blessing

Noah "also said, 'Blessed be the LORD, the God of Shem!' "
(Gen. 9:26). This is a doxology of praise and blessing to the
covenant-keeping God. On account of Shem's piety, his God was
praised as the source of every virtue and good action. It was an
acknowledgment that Shem had a relationship with him. Shem
means "name," as in the sense of having fame. His blessing was in
his identification with Yahweh, the God of the covenant. Note that
his blessing was not due to any external factors. Although Japheth
was the firstborn, Shem and his posterity were preferred over his
older brother as the ones God chose to be their God and recipients
of his covenant blessings.

Through Shem, the promise of God to bring a Redeemer who
would crush the head of Satan would find its fulfillment. As the curse
on Satan in the Garden of Eden brought the promise of blessing
through the Seed of the woman, so the curse on Canaan was the
means for blessing to Shem and ultimately Israel. The blessing came
at one level when Israel conquered the land of Canaan. It would have
further spiritual blessing through the coming of Jesus Christ as a
descendant of Shem, Abraham, and David. When Jesus died on the
cross and rose from the dead, he defeated Satan, crushing his head
(Rom. 16:20; Col. 2:15). Satan's ultimate doom will occur when he
is cast into the lake of fire at the end of this age (Rev. 20:10).

An interesting note of hope for Canaan was found in the blessing.
The blessing was set apart from the curse by the preface, "He also said"
(Gen. 9:26). Although the New International Version translation says,
"May Canaan be the slave of Shem," it could also be translated, "May
Canaan serve him [the God of Shem]" or "Let Canaan be his [God's]
servant" (ESV). This fits within the scope of God's anticipated blessings
going to all peoples as promised to Abram (Gen. 12:3). "Thus both
the wickedness of the Canaanites and God's intended blessing for them

are anticipated in Noah's words."[10] Two Old Testament examples of Canaanites receiving God's blessing are Rahab the prostitute along with her father's household (Josh. 6:25; Heb. 11:31) and the widow of Zarephath of Sidon who was provided for by a miracle through the prophet Elijah during a famine (1 Kings 17:8–16). Sidon was Canaan's firstborn son. A New Testament example is the Canaanite girl from the same region whom Jesus healed because of her mother's great faith (Matt. 15:21–28).

The common blessing on both Shem and Japheth is seen eventually in their embrace of the promises of God and the gospel. Although these blessings do not apply to every individual or family from these two groups, they are fulfilled in an outstanding way from among them.

"May God extend the territory of Japheth" (Gen. 9:27) uses a pun on the words *enlarge* (*yapht*), meaning "to grant ample territory," and *Japheth* (*yepet*). Japheth represents the Gentile nations, many of whom were the Indo-European Aryans (Gen. 10). Almost nothing is said in reference to the Japhethites subsequently in the Old Testament.

Noah's blessing continued: "May Japheth live in the tents of Shem" (Gen. 9:27). This "implies friendly sharing of his hospitality and so of his blessings."[11] It is probably a way of saying, may Japheth share in the blessings given to Shem. A significant event happened in the New Testament when Christ gave the church the mandate to go to all nations with the gospel. The Book of Acts described how the Jewish apostles brought the blessings of the gospel to the Gentiles. They have been grafted into the olive tree of Israel (Rom. 11:17), and they share in Shem's spiritual heritage. It was now a blessing to be brought to all peoples, nations, tribes, clans, and languages. God predicted this in his blessing on Abram, "All peoples on earth will be blessed through you" (Gen. 12:3). This blessing was declared in the Psalms:

May God be gracious to us and bless us
    and make his face shine upon us,
that your ways may be known on earth,
    your salvation *among all nations*.
May the peoples praise you, O God;
    may *all the peoples* praise you.
May the *nations* be glad and sing for joy. (Ps. 67:1–4, emphasis
    added)

We see God's redemptive purposes accomplished through the flow
of biblical history. God is sovereignly in control. Let us now by faith
enter into that blessing and not remain hardened in our hearts, as
were Ham and Canaan. Even the descendants of Ham are called to
enter God's blessing through the promised Seed from Shem.

The curse against Canaan, as the curse on all our sins, can only
be overcome in one way. That is for God himself to take our curse
on him. He did not have to do that. But out of his great love for
his people, he chose to send his Son Jesus Christ to bear our curse
on himself. Jesus "made himself nothing, taking the very nature
of a servant [slave], being made in human likeness. And being
found in appearance as a man, he humbled himself and became
obedient to death—even death on a cross!" (Phil. 2:7, 8). Note
that Jesus took the very role of a slave, which had been Canaan's
curse. "Christ redeemed us from the curse of the law by becoming a curse for us" (Gal. 3:13). The curse of the law is condemnation for our sin. Jesus turned our curse into a blessing for eternity.
In doing that, God the Father exalted him, giving him "the name
that is above every name," making him Lord over heaven and
earth. Someday, "at the name of Jesus every knee should bow"
(Phil. 2:9, 10).

Jesus taught his disciples that "repentance and forgiveness of sins
will be preached in his name to *all* nations" (Luke 24:47, emphasis

added). Paul instructed Gentiles that formerly they "were separate from Christ, excluded from citizenship in Israel and foreigners to the covenants of the promise, without hope and without God in the world. But now in Christ Jesus you who once were far away have been brought near through the blood of Christ" (Eph. 2:12, 13). Through Christ we are made one new people. There is no longer a division or barrier of hostility between Jew and Gentile. We are all reconciled to God through the cross, by which he put to death the hostility between us. Through Jesus "we both have access to the Father by one Spirit" (Eph. 2:18).

Now that the door of faith is open to all, will we not enter God's kingdom where we are all one race, the people of God? Jesus died for all people who will come to him by faith. God's plan is to be gracious to us and to bless us so that his salvation may come to all nations (Ps. 67:1, 2).

SCRIPTURE READING:
EPHESIANS 3:1–13

Discussion Questions

1. Is there ever a time when we can let down our guard against sin? Why or why not?
2. How will you keep yourself from falling into sin, even in old age?
3. What was Ham's sin?
4. Why was Canaan cursed? How has this been fulfilled?
5. What warning must we take from spurning the blessings of the covenant?
6. What is the significance spiritually of the blessing on Shem and Japheth?
7. What hope for blessing do the descendants of Ham have?

Notes

1. Charles R. Erdman, *The Book of Genesis: An Exposition* (Westwood, N.J.: Revell, 1950), 44.

2. James Montgomery Boice, *Genesis,* vol. 1 of *An Expositional Commentary* (Grand Rapids: Zondervan, 1982), 319.

3. John F. Walvoord and Roy B. Zuck, eds., *The Bible Knowledge Commentary,* vol. 1 (Wheaton, Ill.: Victor, 1985), 41.

4. Ibid.

5. Ibid.

6. Ibid.

7. Meredith G. Kline, "Genesis," in *The New Bible Commentary,* ed. D. Guthrie and J. A. Motyer (Grand Rapids: Eerdmans, 1970), 90.

8. Note to the author from Howard Vos.

9. To get a history of racist attitudes against Blacks from ancient times (800 BC to AD 700) see David M. Goldenberg, *The Curse of Ham: Race and Slavery in Early Judaism, Christianity, and Islam* (Princeton, N.J.: Princeton University Press, 2003).

10. John Sailhamer, "Genesis," in vol. 2 of *The Expositor's Bible Commentary,* ed. Frank E. Gaebelein (Grand Rapids: Zondervan, 1990), 97.

11. H. C. Leupold, *Exposition of Genesis,* vol. 1 (Grand Rapids: Baker, 1942), 353.

Book Summary

Discussion Questions

1. What is your view of God through the experience of the Flood and re-creation?
2. Was God justified in his judgment on the world?
3. What is your view of the spiritual condition of humanity and of yourself today?
4. How has God kept his covenant promises?
5. What warning should we beware of in our own day from the Flood?
6. What message of hope do you find throughout the account of Noah's life?
7. How is Noah a model to be emulated in our own lives?
8. How has the gospel been revealed to you, perhaps in a fresh way, through Noah?
9. Respond to the various points of critique of the traditional Christian understanding of God and the Flood account in

the following quotation from a moderated group discussion. This part includes Public Broadcasting System television producer Bill Moyer, journalist Byron (Barney) Calame, and religion writer Karen Armstrong conversing.

Bill: What I meant, Barney, is that if God chose Noah to survive what was to be a carnage, God must have had some purpose beyond our knowing. Maybe He didn't care about the Holocaust and what happened to the six million because He has some other inexplicable purpose. We may not like it. We certainly don't understand it. But there's something at work in the Deity, the Reality beyond our reality, that isn't as intimate with us as most people around this circle would like to imagine.

Barney: I'll buy that.

Karen: But that's thinking about God too much as though He were a human being like us with a personality, writ large, and with likes and dislikes similar to our own.

Bill: I thought I was saying just the opposite—that God may *not* be like us. God may not be moved by Auschwitz.

Karen: No, you're still talking about God as though He were somebody with a plan for the future. It's still anthropomorphic. We need to walk away a little bit from this personalized view of God. In the Noah story, for example, we've got a very personalized God, a God Who starts off by saying He's fed up, He regrets, He's sad in His heart, He wants to change His mind—all the things that God is not supposed to do or be in classical theism. He behaves just like an inadequate human being. The result is that when Noah comes out of his holocaust, he has the blueprint to imitate God and to say he's going to wipe out the people of Canaan. And that continues. So, as I said, perhaps we need to go into the silence for a while. If you look at religious history, you see that in all three of the main traditions of monotheism, monotheists have insisted you have to walk away sometimes from the idea of God as a personality. That's why the Greeks created the doctrine of the Trinity—to remind us that we can't think about God in simple, personal terms.[1]

Note

1. Bill Moyers, *Genesis: A Living Conversation*, ed. Betty Sue Flowers (New York: Doubleday, 1996), 147, 148.

Bibliography

Allis, Oswald T. *God Spake by Moses*. Nutley, N.J.: Presbyterian and Reformed, 1958.

Aquila, Dominic, ed. *PCA News, Information and Resources*. PCANEWS.com (20 August 2002).

Armas, Genaro C. "Record Number of Women Childless," *Philadelphia Inquirer* (25 October 2003), A1.

Baker, William H. *Worthy of Death*. Chicago: Moody, 1973.

Barker, Kenneth, gen. ed. *The NIV Study Bible*. Grand Rapids: Zondervan, 1985.

Barnett, Adrian. www.abarnett.demon.co.uk/atheism/noahs_ark.html (June 2000).

Barnhouse, Donald Grey. *Genesis: A Devotional Exposition*. Vol. 1. Grand Rapids: Zondervan, 1970.

Barrett, David B. and Todd M. Johnson. "Annual Statistical Table on Global Mission: 2003." *International Bulletin of Missionary Research* 27, no. 1 (January 2003): 25.

Berkouwer, G. C. *Man: The Image of God*. Grand Rapids: Eerdmans, 1962.

Boice, James Montgomery. *Genesis*. Vol. 1 of *An Expositional Commentary*. Grand Rapids: Zondervan Publishing Co., 1982.

_____. *Whatever Happened to the Gospel of Grace?* Wheaton, Ill.: Crossway, 2001.

Boice, James Montgomery and Philip Graham Ryken. *The Doctrines of Grace*. Wheaton, Ill.: Crossway, 2002.

Brown, Walt. *In the Beginning: Compelling Evidence for Creation and the Flood*. 7th ed. Phoenix, Ariz.: Center for Scientific Creation, 2001.

Calvin, John. *Commentaries on the First Book of Moses Called Genesis.* Vol. 1. Grand Rapids: Baker, 1999.

DeJong, Norman. *God's Wedding Band.* Winamac, Ind.: Redeemer Books, 1990.

Dilanian, Ken. "Italy Is Baffled by Birth Drop-off." *Philadelphia Inquirer.* (23 December 2002), A8, B.

Duncan, J. Ligon, III. "Covenant of Preservation—Noah," *Covenant Theology* (Jackson, Miss.: First Presbyterian Church, 2000). Audiocassette.

Enda, Jodi. "Lawmakers to Fight for Aid to Population Agency." *Philadelphia Inquirer.* (23 July 2002), A12, C.

Erdman, Charles R. *The Book of Genesis: An Exposition.* Westwood, N.J.: Revell, 1950.

Frame, John M. *No Other God: A Response to Open Theism.* Phillipsburg, N.J.: Presbyterian and Reformed, 2001.

Goldenberg, David M. *The Curse of Ham: Race and Slavery in Early Judaism, Christianity, and Islam.* Princeton, N.J.: Princeton University Press, 2003.

Green, Michael P., ed. *Illustrations for Biblical Preaching.* Grand Rapids: Baker, 1989.

Guralnik, David B., ed. *Webster's New World Dictionary of the American Language.* 2nd ed. Cleveland: Collins, 1979.

Henry, Matthew. *An Exposition of the Old and New Testament.* Vol. 1. Philadelphia: Towar, J. & D. M. Hogan, 1830.

Johnstone, Patrick and Jason Mandryk. *Operation World.* 21st century ed. Waynesboro, Ga.: Paternoster, 2001.

Jukes, Andrew. *Types in Genesis.* Grand Rapids: Kregel, 1976.

Kang, C. H. and Ethel R. Nelson. *The Discovery of Genesis.* St. Louis: Concordia, 1979.

Keil, C. F. and F. Delitzsch. *Commentary on the Old Testament.* Vol. 1. Grand Rapids: Eerdmans, 1975.

Kidner, Derek. *Genesis.* Vol. 1 of *The Tyndale Old Testament Commentaries.* Downers Grove, Ill.: InterVarsity, 1967.

Kline, Meredith G. "Genesis," in *The New Bible Commentary.* Edited by D. Guthrie and J. A. Motyer. Grand Rapids: Eerdmans, 1970.

————. *Kingdom Prologue.* Overland Park, Kans.: Two Age Press, 2000.

Kraus, James, ed. *The Church Around the World* 33, no. 7 (June 2003).

Leary, Warren E. "Found: Possible Pre-Flood Artifacts." *New York Times,* 13 September 2000. International edition.

Leupold, H. C. *Exposition of Genesis.* Vol. 1. Grand Rapids: Baker, 1942.

Link, Mark. *These Stones Will Shout: A New Voice for the Old Testament,* 2nd rev. ed. Allen, Tex.: Argus Communications, 1983.

Louth, Andrew, ed. *Genesis 1–11.* OT vol. 1 of *Ancient Christian Commentary on Scripture.* Downers Grove, Ill.: InterVarsity, 2001.

Marquis, Joshua. " 'Innocents Executed,' a Myth That Deserves Death Penalty." *Philadelphia Inquirer.* (3 January 2002), B, A23.

Millard, Alan. "Flood Stories." In *Eerdmans' Handbook to the Bible.* Edited by David Alexander and Patricia Alexander. Grand Rapids: Eerdmans, 1973.

————. *Treasures from Bible Times.* Belleville, Mich.: Lion, 1985.

Moyers, Bill. *Genesis: A Living Conversation,* ed. Betty Sue Flowers. New York: Doubleday, 1996.

Robertson, O. Palmer. *The Christ of the Covenants.* Phillipsburg, N.J.: Presbyterian and Reformed, 1980.

Ryken, Philip Graham. *My Father's World: Meditations on Christianity and Culture.* Phillipsburg, N.J.: Presbyterian and Reformed, 2002.

Sailhamer, John H. "Genesis." In vol. 2 of *The Expositor's Bible Commentary.* Edited by Frank E. Gaebelein. Grand Rapids: Zondervan, 1990.

Sassone, Robert L. *Handbook on Population.* 3rd ed. N.A., 1973.

Schaeffer, Francis A. *Genesis in Space and Time: The Flow of Biblical History.* Downers Grove, Ill.: InterVarsity, 1972.

Sproul, R. C., ed. *New Geneva Study Bible.* Nashville: Thomas Nelson, 1995.

Unger, Merrill F. *Archaeology and the Old Testament.* Grand Rapids: Zondervan, 1954.

Van Til, Henry R. *The Calvinistic Concept of Culture.* Grand Rapids: Baker, 1972.

Vos, Geerhardus. *Biblical Theology.* Grand Rapids: Eerdmans, 1948.

Vos, Howard F. *Genesis.* Vol. 1 of *Everyman's Bible Commentary.* Chicago: Moody Press, 1982.

Waller, James E. "Deliver Us from Evil: Human Nature and Genocide." *Gordon College Stillpoint* (summer 2003): 11–13.

Walvoord, John F. and Roy B. Zuck, eds. *The Bible Knowledge Commentary.* Vol. 1. Wheaton: Victor, 1985.

Water, Mark, comp. *The New Encyclopedia of Christian Quotations.* Grand Rapids: Baker, 2000.

Whitcomb, John C., Jr. and Henry M. Morris. *The Genesis Flood.* Philadelphia: Presbyterian and Reformed, 1963.

Witsius, Herman. *The Economy of the Covenants between God and Man.* Vol. 2. Reprint, Kingsburg, Calif.: den Dulk Christian Foundation, 1990.

Wong Ming-Dao. Preface and Introduction to *A Stone Made Smooth.* Southampton, Hants, Great Britain: Mayflower, 1981.

Young, Davis A. *The Biblical Flood.* Grand Rapids: Eerdmans, 1995.

————. *Creation and the Flood: An Alternative to Flood Geology and Theistic Evolution.* Grand Rapids: Baker, 1977.

Scripture Index

Hebrews
4:1 — 85, 120
4:3 — 120, 129
4:6 — 86
4:9–11 — 129
4:11 — 86
6:4, 5 — 204
6:8, 9 — 204
9:1–5 — 51
9:13 — 60
9:14 — 60, 152
9:19 — 60
9:22 — 151
10:1 — 65
10:4 — 132
10:9 — 153
10:10 — 132, 137, 153
10:14 — 137
10:22 — 60
10:31 — 54
10:35–39 — 66
11:1 — 65
11:7 — 42, 48, 55, 58, 64, 65, 71, 72
11:10 — 51
11:31 — 206
12:1 — 66
12:2 — 66, 200
12:23 — 18
12:28, 29 — 131
13:8 — 30

James
5:7–11 — 122
5:16 — 133

1 Peter
1:2 — 60
1:4 — 13
1:8 — 67
1:10, 11 — 18
2:13, 14 — 169
2:17 — 169
3:18–22 — 11

3:19 — 18
3:20 — x, 18, 55, 59, 85, 128
3:21 — 55, 59, 85, 128
4:6 — 18
4:8 — 200

2 Peter
2:4 — 11, 13
2:5 — 18, 42, 44, 196
2:9 — 84
2:12 — 147
3 — 123
3:1 — 87
3:3 — 33, 108
3:4 — 33, 108, 188
3:5 — 33, 108, 119
3:6 — 33, 97, 108, 119, 188
3:7 — 33, 55, 108, 119, 188
3:8 — 33, 87
3:9 — 33, 86, 188, 190, 191
3:12 — 33
3:13 — 13, 35

1 John
1:7 — 60, 167, 200
1:9 — 169
2:15–17 — 16
2:18 — 21
3:15 — 167
4:1, 3 — 21
5:3, 4 — 64

2 John
10, 11 — 154

Jude
6 — 11, 13
7 — 11

Revelation
4 — 191
4:3 — 186
5:9 — 76

Subject Index